MARY AND ME

For Patty —
May Mary be an
inspiration on your
journey!
    Best wishes,
        Ginny

MARY AND ME

CATHOLIC

WOMEN

REFLECT

ON

THE

MOTHER

OF

GOD

GINNY KUBITZ MOYER

ST. ANTHONY MESSENGER PRESS
Cincinnati, Ohio

For Mom and Dad,
and for Scott—
Thanks for the unconditional love.

Certain names and identifying details have been changed.

Scripture passages have been taken from *New Revised Standard Version Bible,* copyright ©1989 by the Division of Christian Education of the National Council of the Churches of Christ in the U.S.A., and used by permission. All rights reserved.

Cover and book design by Mark Sullivan.

LIBRARY OF CONGRESS CATALOGING-IN-PUBLICATION DATA
Moyer, Ginny Kubitz.
Mary and me : Catholic women reflect on the Mother of God / by Ginny Kubitz Moyer.
p. cm.
Includes bibliographical references.
ISBN 978-0-86716-831-0 (pbk. : alk. paper) 1. Mary, Blessed Virgin, Saint—Devotion to. 2. Catholic women—Religious life. I. Title.

BT645.M69 2008
232.91—dc22

2007047226

ISBN: 978-0-86716-831-0

Copyright ©2008, Ginny Kubitz Moyer. All rights reserved.

Published by St. Anthony Messenger Press
28 W. Liberty St.
Cincinnati, OH 45202
www.SAMPBooks.org

Printed in the United States of America.

Printed on acid-free paper.

08 09 10 11 12 5 4 3 2 1

| CONTENTS |

| ACKNOWLEDGMENTS |

I want to give my heartfelt thanks to the many people who had a hand in bringing this book into being. The Catherine of Siena Institute's Called and Gifted Workshop set me firmly on the writing path. Bill McGarvey helped shape, flesh out and vastly improve the original BustedHalo.com article on which this book is based. As a classic example of "six degrees of separation," Marjie Murphy provided the critical link that led me to St. Anthony Messenger Press, where Lisa Biedenbach patiently answered my many questions. Mary Curran-Hackett helped call forth and encourage this project when it was still just a gleam in its mommy's eye. Huge hugs to Tarn Wilson, fellow writer and kindred spirit, who read and advised on early drafts. Donna Weiher and Simon Berry generously assisted me in my musical sleuthing.

I want to thank my big sister Amy, who started me on my love of books all those years ago as well as my parents, Alan and Linda Kubitz, who were unflagging in their interest and support, and enthusiastically stepped in with babysitting at critical times. Matthew, my son, provided the inspiration that he alone could give.

My wonderful husband Scott wore oh-so-many hats over the course of this project: editor, tech support, research librarian, project advisor, therapist and general cheerleader. Thank you, Honey. I couldn't have done this without you.

Last, but most certainly not least, a thousand thanks to the many women who shared their stories with me. It's been a privilege—and an absolute joy—to see Mary through your eyes.

| INTRODUCTION |

Like many cradle Catholics, I grew up with a very specific image of Jesus' mother. Mary was a young woman with raised arms, her blue-and-white robes sweeping upward in a graceful arc. Her gaze was downcast, her foot was crushing a serpent. She was beautiful, she was pure and she was everywhere: in my Catholic school classrooms, on the altars of churches, on holy cards and miraculous medals.

Growing up, I loved this image and the woman it represented. For many years, I kept a little picture of Mary in a beige plastic frame on the top of the curio shelf in my bedroom. The picture was a gift from my grade school principal, who had presented me with this token of appreciation after I had spent my fifth grade year helping to run simple errands for her. It seemed only natural to put Mary on the top shelf, above the little china dogs and rabbits and blown-glass deer that I treasured. I felt a quiet admiration for her beauty, her perfection, her lovely face and soft eyes. I knew, instinctively, that she deserved a place of honor, so there she stood for many years, a testament to my respect and affection.

* * *

There's little doubt that the world at large is in love with Mary. Her image is ubiquitous. As a beautiful Renaissance mother, she smiles out of Christmas cards and gazes serenely from the walls of art museums. As a white stone statue, she stands in graceful solitude in flower gardens. As Our Lady of Guadalupe, her image adorns banners, pickup trucks, the sides of buildings. She's even gone Hollywood: Whether it's *The Song of Bernadette* or *The Passion of the Christ*, Mary illuminates the darkness of movie theaters. She truly is the world's most recognizable woman.

Even the plethora of titles by which we know Mary indicates the hold she has on the human heart. The Mother of God, the Ever-Virgin Mary, the Mystical Rose, the New Eve, Queen of the Apostles, Our Lady of Sorrows, Our Lady of Peace; the list goes on and on. Over the centuries, this litany has lengthened as the church has grown in its understanding of Mary's role in our faith tradition. This diverse list of names, fascinating in itself, proves not only the prominence of her place in Catholic tradition, but also the strength of her role in the lives of ordinary Catholics. It seems that Mary has captured the human imagination in a way that few other figures have.

Just as Mary inspires, though, she also polarizes. Other Christian denominations sometimes question her prominence in the Catholic tradition, often resulting in misunderstanding and division. Even within the Catholic church, Mary can be a lightning rod for criticism. Some Catholics feel uncomfortable with Marian devotions, which they see as taking an emphasis away from Christ. Others struggle to understand Marian dogma—the mysteries of the Immaculate Conception and the Assumption. Still other Catholics have deeply held reservations about venerating Mary as a model of womanhood. They wonder how the one woman who was conceived without original sin can be held up as a role model for the rest of us, who will inevitably fall short of her perfection.

This last struggle is one that I know well. As a child, of course, Mary's soft loveliness was an object of admiration; in her tiny plastic frame, she kept watch over my room, high in her place of honor. As I grew older and my horizons expanded, though, I became less and less inclined to keep her in such an exalted position, both in my room and in my heart. Mary's piety, purity and—as I interpreted it—passivity became more and more irritating to me. In college, a time when I was eagerly shedding my Catholic skin, Mary became the symbol of all that I was itching to leave behind. I had no desire for a faith that, in my view, presented women as meekly submissive beings. I had no interest in a faith that told women they had to be virgins, or mothers, or—for goodness' sake!—both at the same time. To me, Mary was the quintessential symbol of a patriarchal faith, one that I was only too happy to leave behind.

In my mid-twenties, though, I started to reengage with Catholicism. The inclusive Catholic community at Stanford University became my spiritual and emotional anchor as I dealt with the rigors of a master's degree program and, later, the challenges of my first teaching job. Over the next few years, the religious learning curve was immense. I was a practicing Catholic again, but this time by choice, not out of habit. I was returning to things that were incredibly familiar, and yet, encountering them anew, I realized that there was more elasticity to Catholicism than I'd ever suspected. My faith and its traditions seemed able to stretch in order to encompass all of my questions, my struggles, my experiences.

In the process, I rediscovered Mary. Over the few years following my reentry into the church, she began, steadily and unmistakably, to stake a claim in my heart. The more profoundly my life changed during that time, the more I was able to connect with her—not as an image on a holy card, not as an impossible standard, but as a real woman whose experiences resonated with my own. When I married my husband, making a commitment to love and honor him all the days of my life, I began to have a new understanding of how Mary must have felt at the Annunciation. Like her, I was saying yes, making a lifelong promise that would transform me in ways I could not possibly anticipate. Like her, I was taking an immense—and yes, even somewhat frightening—leap of faith. Two years later, when I suffered an ectopic pregnancy, the pain I felt was beyond anything I could have expected. For the first time, the image of Mary holding her dead Son spoke to me on a personal level; I had some inkling of the pain she felt at losing her firstborn. Conversely, when I thought of the joy that she felt at discovering her son's Resurrection, it tied in with the emotional closure I eventually found with my own loss. Like her, I found comfort in the certainty that the tiny life inside me was somehow still alive, in the thought that my child was born again in some mysterious way.

Through these experiences and others, I began to truly understand the many faces of Mary and the rich diversity of her roles. That one image of Mary from my childhood was gradually replaced by a host of others. Wife, mother, rejoicer, mourner, disciple, cousin, encourager: I had learned that there truly is a Mary for every moment of my life—and that she was with me every step of the way.

* * *

Over these last few years, I've discovered that there's no lack of published information about Mary. Theologians address her place in Catholic tradition and her role in God's plan of salvation. Numerous authors have written about Marian apparitions, both the famous ones like Lourdes and Guadalupe and lesser-known visitations. Clearly, one could devote a lifetime to studying Mary and still have more to read. Interestingly, though, I've found few titles that look specifically at what I might call the grassroots Mary: at the ways, little or big, that Mary touches the lives of ordinary Catholics. Many times I've found myself pondering a variety of questions, all related to my own shifting experience of the Mother of God. What does Mary mean to Catholic women? Does she challenge, comfort, inspire? Are there certain titles or images of her that resonate strongly with modern women? What are the aspects or moments of Mary's life that are particularly meaningful to women today?

This book began as an article for BustedHalo.com, in which I interviewed Catholic women ages thirty to forty about their thoughts on Mary. Their stories were heartfelt, visceral and real; I was eager to learn more. Again I cast a wide net, inviting women—this time women of all ages—to reflect on their experiences of Mary. Many responded, sharing stories that were thought-provoking, moving and at times unsettling. Their stories form the heart of this book. Woven together, they create a tapestry of ways that Mary speaks to women's lives, a gathering of remembrances and reflections and insights. I've included moments from my own Marian journey as well, a journey that has been enriched immeasurably by the stories I've encountered in researching this book.

Whatever your relationship with Mary, it's my hope that the reflections in this book will give you occasion to ponder her in a new light. I hope that the honesty of these women's stories will inspire you to reflect on your own experience of Mary, and to deepen your understanding of this mother, this woman, this young girl from Galilee whose "yes" has transformed the world.

| ANNUNCIATION: SAYING "YES" |

In the sixth month the angel Gabriel was sent by God to a town in Galilee called Nazareth, to a virgin engaged to a man whose name was Joseph, of the house of David. The virgin's name was Mary. And he came to her and said, "Greetings, favored one! The Lord is with you." But she was much perplexed by his words and pondered what sort of greeting this might be. The angel said to her, "Do not be afraid, Mary, for you have found favor with God. And now, you will conceive in your womb and bear a son, and you will name him Jesus. He will be great, and will be called the Son of the Most High, and the Lord God will give him the throne of his ancestor David. He will reign over the house of Jacob forever, and of his kingdom there will be no end." Mary said to the angel, "How can this be, since I am a virgin?" The angel said to her, "The Holy Spirit will come upon you, and the power of the Most High will overshadow you; therefore the child to be born will be holy; he will be called Son of God. And now, your relative Elizabeth in her old age has also conceived a son; and this is the sixth month for her who was said to be barren. For nothing will be impossible with God." Then Mary said, "Here am I, the servant of the Lord; let it be with me according to your word." Then the angel departed from her. (Luke 1:26–38)

When my parents returned from a recent trip to Italy, my mother remarked on the many artists throughout the years who have found inspiration in Gabriel's visit to Mary. "It seemed like every other painting we saw was a painting of the Annunciation," she told me. Though I'm no art historian, I'd bet that this scene is high on the list of the most popular subjects in Western art. Even a cursory Internet search reveals a staggering number of paintings of this encounter between heaven and earth, this dramatic story told by Saint Luke.

They're lovely, these paintings. In many of them, Mary is depicted as a Renaissance beauty dressed in blue. She holds one hand to her heart, looking downward in an attitude of graceful surprise and surrender. She's usually shown as having been interrupted at some sort of genteel pastime, such as reading. The house in which she sits is sumptuous, with doors opening onto gardens and windows letting in the sky. The artist's perspective, like everything else in the scene, is invariably perfect.

Although I admire these gorgeous Renaissance paintings, I can't help but feel that where the story is concerned, they rather miss the mark. If the painting is too beautiful, too meticulously controlled, it becomes easy to overlook the astonishing nature of the Annunciation. And astonishing it is: A young girl with no particular sense of her own uniqueness is simply going about her business one day. Perhaps she's sweeping, cooking or praying; maybe she's lost in a daydream about her forthcoming marriage. It's life as usual, until out of nowhere comes a creature the likes of which she's never seen, with a proposal utterly unlike anything she's ever imagined. Greatly perplexed, she hears him out. It's a defining moment for Mary: Will she embrace what the angel is saying? Will she accept this incredible idea that she will be the Mother of God? Will she beat back her doubt and agree to walk this path, a path that will lead to goodness knows where?

She does. Somehow, this young girl looks at the incomprehensible future offered to her, makes herself larger than her fear, and says: I'll take it.

* * *

Several of the women I interviewed tried to imagine what Mary must have been feeling at the Annunciation, both during and after this surprise encounter. "I wonder if Mary had a few moments of wonder and maybe even second thoughts after Gabriel's visit, where she questioned what had just happened," reflects Donna, a fifty-six-year-old elementary school music teacher. "Sort of like, 'Whoa! What did I just do? Oh, brother!

How am I gonna explain this to Joseph and my parents?'" Though Donna doesn't believe that Mary ever regretted her "yes," she does find it hard to understand that Mary would accept such a mysterious mission without requesting more time to think it through. "I say that because I process information slowly, and it takes me some time to work through things. I wonder if Mary had some moments of questioning after this amazing event."

Donna's thoughts touch on a crucial aspect of the story: Mary accepts God's plan with remarkable quickness and with very little information on which to base her decision. Her one question is, "How can this be?" to which Gabriel responds that the Holy Spirit will come upon her, and the power of the Most High will overshadow her. It's a response that, for most of us, I imagine, provides far more questions than answers. The angel also says nothing about how Mary will weather the storm of public opinion, surely a question that must have crossed her mind. After all, she agreed to something that no one in her town could possibly have been expected to understand. As an unmarried pregnant woman, she was opening herself to harsh gossip and ridicule, even to death under the Mosaic Law. Agreeing to put herself in such a precarious position was nothing less than astonishing. To agree to this so quickly is all the more radical.

To Alice, a sixty-one-year-old kindergarten teaching aide, this ready acceptance is deeply inspiring. "She accepted her path to God even though it caused, I'm sure, great embarrassment to her and to her family. She had to do what she knew to be right, in spite of what her friends and neighbors thought of her. What courage she exhibited! I admire that courage so much." Alice goes on to say that even though she herself has not had the experience Mary has, "I can relate to how hard it is to stand by your beliefs against today's accepted standards." Though the classic paintings of the Annunciation often present Mary bending in graceful humility, Alice's words paint a picture of a girl with a formidable backbone. This is no passive Mary, but a woman who courageously took a huge personal risk, all in the name of faith.

It's a faith that is all the more inspiring because of Mary's youth. Most Bible scholars believe that Mary was a young teenager at the time of Gabriel's visit—a fact that can be hard to remember given the womanly and mature look of so many of her portraits. Thinking about it in modern terms, Mary was not old enough to vote, not even old enough to have a driver's license, when she accepted this life-altering mission.

Several of the women I talked to remarked on this, marveling at the fact that a girl who was barely out of puberty could have such radical faith. "She was so young when she was asked to carry a child that was to live and die for humankind," says Andrea, a thirty-three-year-old marriage and family therapy intern and school counselor. "That is hard to fathom at my present age, let alone as a teenager." Andrea's connection to Mary is deeply personal, going back to her second grade year, when the Catholic school she attended put on a Nativity pageant. "Roles were selected by drawing names. I selected Mary and I remember all of the other girls wanting to trade with me. That is when I realized that Mary was someone special." Now, as an adult, Andrea has a more mature and nuanced understanding of exactly what makes this woman so special. "Mary strikes me as simple in a grand way. She followed through with the work of God and demonstrated how to do this with faith. She may not have originally understood why she was chosen to be the mother of Jesus but she did what was asked of her." Andrea believes Mary's response to the call "shows how we as modern women can act on our faith even if we cannot understand what is being asked of us."

Sister Patricia, I.H.M., a sixty-year-old formation education consultant, author and public speaker, has also found inspiration in the depth of Mary's faith. Her relationship with Mary began in childhood: In elementary school she had a Marian shrine in her bedroom, loved the hymns of Mary she sang at her school and in fourth grade announced that she would become a religious sister when she grew up. "On the spot I exacted the promise of my father that he would buy me a very large statue of Mary for my first classroom, emphasis on the world *large*," Sister Patricia recalls.

But in spite of this childhood admiration, she lacked a true personal connection to Mary. "In childhood Mary was to me the holy mother of Jesus and I lumped her into the category of all moms. We did not share an intimacy. She was *there* and I was *here*."

It was in her teenage years that Sister Patricia found herself connecting with Mary in a more meaningful way. "Mary became more personal because I made the connection that she was a teenager like me when Gabriel's message and her response to it turned her world inside out. I saw her as an adolescent who must have had dreams and hopes for her future before Gabriel's arrival! And yet she willingly turned everything over to God. It dawned on me that her attitude toward God and the will of God was not an overnight phenomenon but that it *had* to have represented the pattern of her behavior choices up to that moment." To Sister Patricia this realization helped her internalize Mary's courage. "That reality caused me to admire Mary. I saw the value of following her example in openness to and readiness for God."

It's clear from my interviews that even though the Annunciation took place two thousand years ago, these women can imagine it as vividly as if it happened yesterday. Whether they feel admiration for Mary's courage or awe at her swift "yes," many modern women can't help but become personally engaged in her experience. In a way, that's not surprising, for the Annunciation is far more than just one girl's story; it's an encounter that has the power to speak to all women everywhere. Through Mary's response, we're reminded that some truly amazing things can happen when we let faith overcome our fear.

* * *

Perhaps another reason why the Annunciation is so compelling to women today is because every one of us can, on some level, relate to Mary's moment of decision. Though she's the only one in history who has been offered the chance to become the Mother of God, the process of navigating our way through life's choices is universal to humankind. Like Mary, every one of us has had the experience of being at a turning point in life, pondering the options that lie before us.

Sometimes the issue at hand is personal: Do I break up with my fiancé or hope we can resolve our problems? How do I deal with my teenage son's rebellion? Should I put my mother into assisted living? Other times, it's professional: Do I stay at home with the kids or go back to work? I just quit the job that I hated—now what do I do? Many times, these questions have a spiritual dimension. Standing at the point where two or more paths diverge, we hunger for guidance. *Okay, God*, we pray, *if you really do have a plan for me, I'd love to know what it is.* Whether it's with patience, frustration or resignation, we wait for some sort of sign, some stirring in the soul, that will give us the clarity not only to discern but also embrace the life we are called to live.

And, as I learned from several of the women I interviewed, sometimes it's Mary herself who points the way. Through two stories in particular, it becomes clear that Mary herself sometimes steps into our confusion, giving us the confidence to say yes.

* * *

"The Blessed Mother had a *very* direct influence on my religious vocation," says Sister Rose Martin, O.P. The eighty-two-year-old retired grade school teacher recalls a time in her early twenties, before entering the convent, when she worked as a teletype operator for Western Union. "Those were happy days of friends, dates, steady salary, freedom, use of the family car, socials and youthful activities," she says. "All the while, I was looking, but not searching, for that God-sent, faith-filled man who would be my life's mate." Though there were many boyfriends, somehow the right man never quite came along.

It was around age twenty-four that she began to feel the need for a deliberate discernment of her true calling. As part of this process, she began to stop at her parish church to pray on the way home from work. It was there one evening that she found a small vocation holy card that seemed to symbolize her own search. "On the card was the figure of a person standing on a road that had three joining roads; one led to married life, another to the single life and another road to the religious life. The searching figure's simple image immediately became my position and my prayer. 'Lord, I stand before you with this prayer—please, somehow, let me know your will for my path. I firmly resolve to say this prayer every day, begging you to help me understand what *you* wish for my life's service to you." It was a prayer that she prayed in church every evening, before the statue of Mary.

Weeks went by, and the visits to church became longer, the prayers more intense. As Rose explains, she was sure that someday she would have a clear answer. Standing at a crossroads, she was ready to take whichever path God indicated. "It didn't matter what he would ask of me, I trusted his goodness."

As time passed, the religious life began to figure more prominently in her thoughts. It occurred to Rose that she should begin preparing her mother for the possibility that she might become a sister. One day, she took the plunge. "She and I were standing in the kitchen, and I didn't want to face my mother when I told her, so I turned toward the oven and casually said, 'Mom, perhaps I won't get married, maybe I'll enter a convent.' To my total shock her immediate answer was, 'Rose, I'm not surprised. I could see it coming.' God was making the religious life path more clear each day!"

In spite of the little nudges she was feeling, Rose needed a more positive assurance that this was her call. She decided to make a weekend retreat at the Dominican College in San Rafael, California. Late one evening, in the chapel, she knelt before the statue of Mary. "I poured out my heart in tears and begged her to help me understand God's will—what path did he want me to follow?" Though she was still crying when she left, she felt certain that Mary would let her know God's plan.

On her way back to the dorm where she was staying, she took a path that wound through a very dark garden. "Being so filled with divine peace, I made my way along the path. Suddenly, clearly, loudly, I heard my name—'ROSE!' Thinking that one of my friends was calling me, I retraced my steps along the darkened path. But no one was there! Words cannot describe my awakening surprise and total openness to God's call." Arriving at the dorm room, she burst into what she called "joyous tears of love, humility, awe and wonder." This, she realized, was the "wake-up call" she had wanted.

Having felt the call to religious life, she needed to discern which community to join. Not knowing much about any religious orders, she decided to explore the life of the Dominican sisters at her parish. She knocked at the convent door one day, and when a sister answered, Rose asked her for information about the order. The sister welcomed her, invited her in and asked Rose her name. When she responded, "Rose Martin," the sister gasped and hurriedly left the room.

Perplexed by her reaction, Rose waited. When the sister returned, she was accompanied by all of the religious sisters in residence at the convent. Rose recalls, "They told me the exciting news that at that very week, all of the fourteen postulants at the motherhouse in Mission San Jose were praying to Saint Martin, a Dominican lay brother, for another postulant to bring their number up to fifteen, as in fifteen decades of the Dominican rosary." Rose was as astonished as they were—the fact that her last name was that of the saint to whom the sisters were praying felt like far more than mere coincidence. "To me, *that* was a miracle! And to learn that my first name, Rose, is also the name of a Dominican saint was just an overwhelming surprise and joy!" Visits to the order's motherhouse later helped Rose confirm that her life's path was one she would walk as a Dominican sister.

For Rose, there's no doubt that Mary's intercession helped her identify and say "yes" to the life she was meant to live. "My decision to enter that convent on Our Lady's Feast, December 8, was to me the crowning point of a long search, a heavenly gift," she says. "It was the beginning of a joyous life of praise and thanksgiving to our Lady, sweet Mystical Rose."

* * *

As Sister Rose discovered there are times when life presents us with a clear crossroads. The paths are well-marked, displayed before our eyes; it's simply a matter of discerning which one to follow. But what happens when the future is not a crossroads, but a maze? What do we do when we can't even see what our options are? How do we proceed when we know our current lifestyle isn't working for us, but we have no idea where to go from there?

Beth, a forty-eight-year-old director of sales for the HBO network, knows this struggle well. Six years ago, her high-stress job was draining her, making her physically and emotionally exhausted. Though she had no idea how to find a new direction in life, she soon discovered that Mary was guiding her back to something she hadn't even known she was missing: the faith she had given up twenty-five years before.

Growing up, religion was something that Beth experienced through parochial schools and Mass on Sundays. As a child, she recalls that she didn't feel particularly connected to Catholicism; though her mother always had rosaries about the house, faith was never something her family discussed. It was simply something they did.

It was as a freshman in college that Beth began to think more consciously about her religious identity. Though she attended a Catholic school, she recalls that Catholic students were in the minority; Beth was meeting her first Jews, atheists, Buddhists. "I was intrigued that the world was so much bigger than I knew it was," she explains. "It was not cool to be Catholic, even on a Catholic university campus, and I was all about being cool. I really wanted to fit in." Freshman year, she stopped going to Mass, and, as she explains, gave it no thought for the next twenty-five years. "I didn't miss it, didn't try on any other religions and just felt very absent from any need to have, or take an interest in, a relationship to God."

During that period of distance from her faith, her family was touched by tragedy: In 1993, Beth's brother Erik died of AIDS. Shortly after his death Beth recalls that her mother came home one day with a huge statue of Mary. "She borrowed it from the church or something, brought it home, and put it in the living room. I remember looking at it and thinking, 'How ridiculous.'" Because they never discussed their faith, Beth's mother had no idea that her daughter had stopped going to Mass. "She said to me, not knowing how I felt about anything, 'Isn't it comforting to have Mary here with us, like this, in this statue?'" Beth said nothing in response, but felt, as she put it, "filled with disgust. I thought, 'No, it's not, it's a stupid statue, what's that supposed to do?' I couldn't even look at her, I was so annoyed with the whole concept."

Seven years later, Beth was working for a high-tech firm in Silicon Valley. She was miserable: The job was high-powered and extremely stressful, and within a few years, it began taking a huge toll on her emotional and physical health. "For about one year, I'd been waking up every morning about two, three, four AM with back spasms that would make it difficult for me to breathe," she explains. "I literally had to fall on the floor out of bed and crawl to the bathroom or somewhere to get comfortable." Each night was such a trial to her that she used to cry even at the thought of getting into bed, knowing the pain that awaited her.

One night, at the recommendation of a massage therapist, she took a particularly hot bath and went straight to bed. As she lay in bed, a blue light entered her room, initially appearing as a flash across the foot of her bed. Beth thought at first that it was an aftereffect of the extremely hot bath she'd just taken. "Then the light took a shape right above me, like a cone, with the smallest point away from me, and then the biggest point closest to me, spinning like a vortex. I remember looking at it and thinking I didn't want to blink or breathe—there was something going on here." She describes the light as being the most exquisite shade of blue. There were no words or sound coming from the light, but somehow Beth felt the words, "Everything's going to be all right." She fell asleep, and for the first time in a long while, slept through the night. The mysterious light had brought her a feeling of much-needed peace and solace, though she recalls, "I didn't at the time associate it with Mary. It nevertheless comforted me."

As powerful as this experience was, Beth knew she still needed to make a drastic change to regain her emotional health. A few months later, she quit her job, sublet her apartment, packed her bags and got into her car. She didn't know where she was going and had no timeline or agenda for her road trip. Only one thing was clear: She was at a turning point, and needed to find a new life for herself.

For the next five months, she drove all the way from California to Nova Scotia and back. Though she had no conscious itinerary or purpose, she soon discovered one: visiting churches. Without knowing why, she found herself stopping her car in front of Catholic churches in different states. "I'd see a Catholic church as I was driving through Town X, and I'd pull over, and stop, and I'd walk in. I'd feel embarrassed and agitated— thank God I'm in Utah, Wyoming, Montana, where no one knows me, because I don't want anyone to see me going into a Catholic church." She had no idea why she was doing it, but felt "compelled from the outside in." It was only when she'd arrive in the vestibule of the church that it would hit her: She was there because she was looking for Mary.

Inside the church, Beth would look for a statue of Mary. If the church did not have one, she left. "If there was a statue," she recalls, "I'd make a beeline for it, and I'd hit my knees and just bawl, and have no idea what I was doing, but I do remember that my only recurring prayer was, 'OK, clearly you have something to do with my being here, because I don't know why I'm here. I don't know if I believe in you, I don't know if I believe in your son, but obviously, what I'm doing is not working for me. I'm miserable, so if you have something to say to me, please hit me over the head. Woman to woman,' I'd say, 'I have to hear it from a woman, because I just can't hear it otherwise.'" There was no message coming back, Beth recalls, but she kept praying all the same. "I was looking for Mary all across the United States—not interested in going to Mass, just hanging out with statues."

When her trip took her through Colorado, she decided to look up a former boyfriend who had become a Trappist monk. She checked into the guest facilities at the monastery and planned to stay only one day. It felt uncomfortable to be in the presence of so many monks: "I felt like I was a fraud. I wouldn't want to have to have a conversation with any of them, because I wasn't a believer."

Jeff, her friend, eventually coaxed her out of the hermitage. She ended up staying an entire week, and found herself confiding her Mary search to him. He introduced her to a monk with a strong devotion to Mary, but their conversation left Beth feeling ill at ease. "He said, 'Say the rosary every day, Mary is calling you to be holy, she is calling you to be bigger than the person that you were. Listen to her, follow her lead.' I just felt uncomfortable with the whole thing." The day before she left, though, she felt compelled to ask the abbot to hear her confession. It didn't feel like a conscious decision, more like something motivated by someone else. It was a decision that was all the more strange because Beth had not yet decided whether she wanted to return to her faith. She recalls, "I said to the priest, 'I really don't know why I'm doing this, but I feel compelled to do this now. It's been a remarkable week, but I don't know if I'm willing to follow through.'" After that confession, though, she went to Mass, and received Communion for the first time in twenty-five years, an experience that she describes as being full of joy and peace.

Back home, resolved to continue exploring this faith journey, Beth walked into a church whose Gothic architecture intrigued her. Sitting in the pew, she noticed a card advertising the Landings program, a program for returning Catholics who want to explore the possibility of reconnecting with the church. On the card was a picture of a rose, a flower which Beth had always associated with Mary. It was this little push that helped motivate her to explore the Landings program, in spite of some significant doubts. "I was very nervous about that, not sure I wanted to commit, not sure why I was doing any of it." Her reservations about reengaging with the church came partly from her experiences with her brother. "One of the things I was most anxious about was talking about the church's position on homosexuality," she recalls. "I was still in something of a throw-the-baby-out-with-the-bathwater phase regarding participation in the church."

Before beginning the Landings process, each potential returnee is interviewed by a practicing Catholic. Much to Beth's surprise, the man who interviewed her revealed that he too had lost a brother to AIDS. "I thought that was the last sign I needed, that I was supposed to be there," she recalls. "It's just like that first message I got in my bedroom. 'Everything's going to be OK.'" Through the Landings program, Beth was empowered to reconnect with the practice of her faith. Now, years later, she is an active and involved member of her parish community.

Beth's sense of God is that he speaks many languages in order to connect with his people. For her, Mary was the language he used to call her home. Interestingly, she finds her relationship with Mary has shifted since her reentry into the church. "I do feel like as the years unfold, she gets quieter and Christ's voice gets louder inside of me, which of course is the point. But she's still there, and my prayers are more often ones of gratitude toward her. When my other female friends are suffering, I ask her to comfort them the way she has comforted me, with that blue light, or whatever it is, if that was her. Everybody should have it."

As Beth sees it now, Mary represented a comfort that she needed to feel in order to make the choice to reengage with her faith. Beth muses, "I don't see her as the source of any answers, only 100 percent comfort so I can relax, stop panicking and look up for an answer—for a dialogue," she explains. "But I know I can't start that dialogue if I'm freaked out and anxious, and that's why I think the comfort factor is so important." Reflecting on her attitude toward Mary—and Christ—back in 2000, she recognizes why she counted on Mary, rather than Christ. "I couldn't go to Christ directly. It was too intimidating to start there," she says. Since then, she explains, she has come to see Christ as a source of solace in her life, but "he's also the source of many challenges—accountability, authority and consequences. He's teacher, master and judge. Mary is only comfort. Mary is only love—and a beautiful way to get to her son, maybe especially for women."

Throughout her life, Beth explains, it's her female friends who have played a critical role. "It's my women friends who make the real difference in my life and always have. I don't even know what I would do without my women friends." For Beth the knowledge that there was a woman waiting inside was the catalyst to step not only into churches across the country, but back into the church as a whole. It was Mary's female nature that helped Beth identify and say her own "yes" to a journey of faith that still astonishes her. Beth's prayer to statues across the country sums up the reason for her journey and reveals the power of having Mary as a guide:

Mary,
As a woman,
help me understand,
help me see,
because I don't see—
but I'm open to anything you have to say.

* * *

There's a power in sharing our human experiences, and nowhere is this more true than in matters of faith. Although I have a deep appreciation for the beautiful artistic renderings of the Annunciation, it's these women's reflections that make this scene most fully alive for me. Through each others' stories, we have a chance to see the dynamism of Mary, and to understand how she lives and breathes in the lives of women today, two thousand years after her own astonishing leap of faith.

And, in the end, Mary's "yes" challenges me to think about my own way of dealing with life's turning points. In the mini-annunciations of my own life, how do I respond? I'm a long way from having her faith, but I like to think that in those moments when I stand at a crossroads, she's there for me, as she is for all of us, a heavenly champion who nudges us toward our greatest joy. "I said 'yes' to what God offered me," Mary seems to say, "and I've never regretted it. Neither will you."

| VISITATION: THE JOURNEY INTO COMMUNITY |

In those days Mary set out and went with haste to a Judean town in the hill country, where she entered the house of Zechariah and greeted Elizabeth. When Elizabeth heard Mary's greeting, the child leaped in her womb. And Elizabeth was filled with the Holy Spirit and exclaimed with a loud cry, "Blessed are you among women, and blessed is the fruit of your womb. And why has this happened to me, that the mother of my Lord comes to me? For as soon as I heard the sound of your greeting, the child in my womb leaped for joy. And blessed is she who believed that there would be a fulfillment of what was spoken to her by the Lord."

And Mary said,
"My soul magnifies the Lord,
*   and my spirit rejoices in God my Savior,*
for he has looked with favor on the lowliness of his servant.
*   Surely, from now on all generations will call me blessed;*
for the Mighty One has done great things for me,
*   and holy is his name.*
His mercy is for those who fear him
*   from generation to generation.*
He has shown strength with his arm;
*   he has scattered the proud in the thoughts of their hearts.*
He has brought down the powerful from their thrones,
*   and lifted up the lowly;*
he has filled the hungry with good things,
*   and sent the rich away empty.*
He has helped his servant Israel, in remembrance of his mercy,
according to the promise he made to our ancestors,
*   to Abraham and to his descendants forever."*
And Mary remained with her about three months and then returned to her home. (Luke 1:39-56)

At the age of thirty-three, I'm fortunate to live near five of the women who were my closest friends in high school. The history we've shared has been varied, to say the least. As teenagers we shared hair spray and English notes and painfully extracted confessions about which boy we liked. Then came graduation, and we radiated out in all directions for college, study-abroad programs, jobs and graduate school. In our late teens and early twenties, we shared our diverse experiences through letters and phone calls and we made an effort to get together during vacations when we returned home. Now we're all settled back in the Bay Area, so we manage to meet once a month for dinner (in spite of our hectic schedules). At these meetings our conversations usually cover a range of topics: career crises and triumphs, dating and marriage, pregnancies both planned and unexpected, struggles with infertility and child-rearing, the challenge of navigating the real estate market. We've attended each other's weddings and housewarmings and baby showers, events that would have seemed incomprehensible to our high school selves. Over the years we've processed, shared and analyzed countless romantic relationships; we've tried gamely to put a positive spin on the ones that ended, and have celebrated the ones that were right after all. In other words, we've been community to each other through the good, the bad and everything in between.

It's thanks to friendships like these that I can understand the essence of the Visitation. In this Gospel story, two women come together, each with her own experience to share. Mary comes ready to discuss her miraculous visitor and the pregnancy that no doubt still astonishes her. Greeting her at the door, Elizabeth has her own story to tell—the shocking fact that she has conceived a child after having resigned herself to a life of infertility. What a relief each of them must have felt to be with another woman, one who could not only understand the physical experience of pregnancy, but who could marvel in the power that made it all possible. Two women, one too old to conceive, the other still a virgin, both expecting a child—that's the kind of experience that needs to be processed, shared, analyzed, and, most of all, celebrated.

But before the celebration comes the journey: Mary's journey into community.

* * *

The Bible says that Elizabeth lived in a "hill town" in Judea, and that it was to this place that Mary traveled "in haste." To me this landscape sounds appealing. I think of the hills that divide my city from the ocean twenty miles away. Driving through them is not only scenic but comfortable thanks to the paved roads and my car's plush seats. Because of this, it's a stretch for me to understand what Mary's journey would have been like.

In his book *A New Testament Guide to the Holy Land,* John J. Kilgallen, S.J., identifies Mary's destination as the town of Ein Karem, a town eighty miles south of Nazareth.[1] Eighty miles of hilly terrain, most likely traveled either by foot or on a donkey: This was hardly a pleasant afternoon outing, but a trek that took significant stamina. Pictures of this region show a bleak, desolate land, with scrubby or nonexistent vegetation. It looks far from inviting for any traveler, particularly a woman in the early stages of pregnancy.

For Karen, a thirty-six-year-old attorney, the fact that Mary willingly took on such a formidable landscape is more than just an interesting aspect of the Visitation story. In fact, Mary's journey has played a critical role in helping Karen connect with Mary as a woman and a role model. It's a bond that Karen never felt in her younger years, a time when her understanding of the Mother of God was limited at best. "My childhood thoughts of Mary were rather superficial," she recalls. "Of course, she was supposed to be incredibly beautiful, and that was certainly appealing to a young girl. But beyond that, I never thought much about her."

This indifference changed when Karen was a teenager and became friends with several born-again Christians. Though she continued to attend Mass with her family, she felt herself questioning the traditions and beliefs of her childhood faith. "I saw the Catholic faith as obsessively focused on religion, ritual and superstition, rather than faith in Jesus.

Mary became a lightning rod in my mind for all that I considered to be wrong with the church." In fact, Karen explains, she became "particularly incensed by what I saw as the 'hocus-pocus' factor—the belief that God would listen if you said particular prayers to Mary or wore a particular medal. I didn't understand why people would pray to Mary if they could just go directly to Jesus."

In college Karen happened upon a Catholic church that had a vibrant young adults' community. It was a turning point in her faith journey. "People I met there encouraged me to ask questions about all aspects of the Catholic faith," she explains. "I gradually came to understand the Catholic church's teachings about Mary (which I had never really learned before), and I began to appreciate Mary's role in the faith." In spite of this renewed Catholic identity, Karen still lacked a personal relationship with the Mother of God.

All that changed in 1998 when Karen made a pilgrimage to the Holy Land. There, she traveled over the route Mary would have taken to visit Elizabeth. "As I looked at that long and difficult path, I realized what a strong and courageous woman Mary must have been," Karen explains. "While Mary is often portrayed as meek and submissive, I suspect that she was actually very brave, active and even a little gritty. Here she was, a young woman who understood what it would mean to be an unwed mother in a highly restrictive society, but nonetheless bravely said 'yes' when asked to be the Mother of God—not the conduct of a meek wallflower. Then, rather than sit around worrying about what she will do, she picks up and walks on a long journey to be with her cousin Elizabeth." To Karen this plucky, active Mary is far more compelling than the traditional portrayal of "a beautiful, porcelain-faced woman with downcast eyes. That's never been a role model for me. But I am much more taken with the image I gained in Israel of a strong-willed, courageous woman, who defied convention and bravely did the will of God. I would love to see women reclaim Mary in this light."

For Karen the pilgrimage was more than just a journey to the Holy

Land —it was a journey into a more intimate connection with the woman who gave birth to the son of God. "I now find myself occasionally praying to Mary, particularly since I became a mother," she explains. "It is the image of Mary setting out on her journey to see Elizabeth that I usually think of—not the image in all the paintings, but an image of a real, normal woman (OK, not completely normal, but able to relate to normal women) who can relate to my life. My prayers to her are generally for strength and peace during trying times. I figure she knows a lot about that." Ultimately, Karen finds resonance in the image of a woman who walked a difficult path in order to fulfill her destiny, and in the meantime, helped a beloved cousin fulfill hers.

* * *

Many artistic depictions of the Visitation focus on the same moment: Mary and Elizabeth standing at the threshold of the house, greeting each other with an embrace. Familial bonds, mutual affection, a shared past, present and future—all are expressed through these two women and their open arms. It's a rare glimpse into the network of Mary's extended family, revealing the depth of her love for her cousin. On a larger level, this embrace symbolizes more than just a blood relationship. It represents an openness to community and a willingness to be present to those in need.

It's the symbolism of this meeting that resonates with Sister Kristin, a Dominican sister of San Rafael. "The Mary and Elizabeth Visitation, in which they reach out and support one another, is what we are all called to do—to reach out and support one another, and, I would add, particularly those who are poor and the homeless," says the sixty-eight-year-old clinical psychologist and former prioress. In her own life she has learned firsthand what it means to be on both the giving and receiving end of such generosity. It was the spirit of the Visitation that guided her and her fellow sisters through two painful losses, ultimately reinvigorating their community.

In 1989, Saint Rose Academy, the San Francisco school that was run by the sisters, was destroyed in the Loma Prieta earthquake. The sisters were still recovering from that loss when, one year later, their century-old motherhouse in nearby San Rafael was destroyed by fire. Though no one was hurt, the sisters lost the uninhabitable building as well as many possessions. The sisters were, in a word, *homeless*.

In the wake of this tragedy came an outpouring of goodwill. Other sisters came from all over Northern California with as many cars as they could to take back the women who had been displaced. "People came down with every intention of doing whatever needed doing so that the sisters could have a roof over their heads," recalls Sister Kristin. "It was a very powerful experience, in all honesty." Years later, she still marvels at the emotional impact of seeing so many women come together. "It was sort of like we had been through this terrible thing—actually, two terrible things, we lost Saint Rose, then the motherhouse—but people didn't get wigged out about it. People took care of one another. And I think that's what tuned me into Mary going to visit Elizabeth…in the embrace of one another, we knew we were cared for."

Even beyond the outpouring of hospitality, the tragedy of the fire pulled the sisters together in a new way. Following the devastation, the community had a decision to make: Should they rebuild the old motherhouse or should they tear it down and start over? They held a meeting to decide the issue and "almost every sister who was able to walk came to it," recalls Sister Kristin. When the vote was finally taken, the community was of one accord: out of 175 sisters, 173 of them wanted to start over, with two abstaining from the vote. Not a single sister voted to rebuild.

It took five long years to build the new motherhouse, but in 1995, it was time to move in. At the opening of the sisters' new home, Sister Kristin gave a talk in which she reflected upon the lessons learned from the fire. "If our encounters clarify for us what God is calling us to be and do," she told her community, "then truly our encounters are holy, and we will become holier in the struggle to clarify our shared vision and common values." Those words have clearly had a lasting impact on her community, for when Sister Kristin finished her final term as prioress, her fellow sisters had the lines printed on a large framed copy of one of her favorite paintings, which is a portrait of the Visitation by Fra Angelico. The picture now hangs in a place of honor in her room.

The holiness of encountering others has always guided Kristin's education and ministry. She holds a PH.D. in psychology, and for fourteen years she worked in a hospital psychiatric ward, a job to which she felt a great calling. As she explains, she has always been drawn to "work with people who are poor at the level of human existence—and no one is more poor at the level of human existence than a psychotic individual." In an echo of Mary's Magnificat, she reflects, "I wouldn't want to work in a position where I was with people of power and prestige, and treated well, because those aren't the people who are even seeking help. What I knew was I did want to work with people who are poor at the level of existence, and for whom there weren't a lot of people helping them." This desire has led to her current position: counseling women who are drug-addicted and involved in prostitution. Most of her work involves one-on-one therapy, in which she meets with the women and does what she calls the "Mary and Elizabeth thing." "I think there's a magic in women coming together, in which they can really touch one another at a deeply meaningful core, and bring out the best in one another," she reflects. "I see that sometimes in the women I work with—when they sense they're cared about, they'll open up; they'll talk, and they'll cry. I think they can hear your message of, 'You're going to have to figure out how to get off of drugs.' " Such personal support, she explains, is crucial to helping others transform their lives. "In the depths of your heart, you can achieve what you want to get, but we can't do it by ourselves—it's not solitary. We can be Mary to Elizabeth, or we can be Elizabeth embracing Mary, either one—but it's in that moment that we enable one another to stay the course, to do the hard thing, to do what we know needs doing." She acknowledges that it's not always easy; sometimes these encounters involve reaching beyond our own comfort zones. "Human beings can touch the heart of one another, but they have to give up something of themselves to do that. They have to take a risk sometimes to challenge the other, or to disappoint the other in some way. It's in those moments that I think God is within us."

If there's one thing that Sister Kristin has learned, both through her work and her community, it's that unexpected challenges can be a catalyst for growth. Nowhere was this more evident than in the fire and its aftermath, which "brought the sisters together in a way that nothing else could have done." She suspects that the experience helped many of her fellow sisters reconnect with the spirit of the Visitation, sensing that "maybe it deepened their own sense of commitment to their vows, to serving the people of God." In the end, she reflects, the tragic loss of the motherhouse became a priceless gift: a vivid reminder of what it means to be a community. "I think that happens in life sometimes," she muses. "The thing that seems so devastating ends up being the gift—the opening of a new vision."

* * *

In my own life, too, devastation has led to an intimate understanding of the Visitation. In the fall of 2004, I became pregnant with my first child. My husband, Scott, and I were thrilled—overwhelmed by the enormity of our new vocation, but thrilled all the same. Children had always been a part of the life we'd envisioned for ourselves, and those two bold lines on the pregnancy test were proof that we were on our way.

Within a week, though, troubling signs began to appear. I was bleeding lightly, and even more worrisome were the waves of pain I felt on my right side, pain that would begin steadily, then crest to such a level that I'd have to brace myself until it subsided. I called the doctor, who ordered blood tests and ultrasounds. One week later, we learned that it was an ectopic pregnancy, which occurs when the embryo implants itself outside of the uterus where it has no chance of survival.

The next few days passed in a daze of doctor's visits and unfamiliar medical terminology. My joy had turned so quickly to sorrow that I felt utterly disoriented. It was all wrong, as if a rug had been whisked out from under my feet; I'd lost my emotional footing. I mourned the death of that little life inside me, one which had had to end before it had barely begun.

We told our closest friends about our loss, and their sympathetic e-mails, cards and phone calls did much to help. Still there was an ache inside me that nothing could alleviate—not prayer, not good wishes, not even Scott's tight embraces. Though he too was devastated by our loss, the fact that it had happened within my own body made me feel the grief in a visceral way that he could not understand. I felt very alone in my pain.

Nearly four weeks after this loss, and one week before my regular dinner with my high school friends, I received an e-mail from my friend Liz. She was writing to tell me that she was pregnant, and was hoping to announce her good news at our dinner. She had wanted to tell me in advance, she explained, for she felt that it would be easier for me to have some prior warning. Very kindly, she offered to hold back from telling everyone at dinner if it would be too painful a reminder of my own loss.

As happy as I was for her, I can't deny that her news felt like salt on a raw wound. Her due date was only a month behind what mine would have been; the closeness of the timing only underscored my own loss. I couldn't help but feel a sense of envy, and the sorrow of being unable to make my own excited announcement to our group of friends. Still, I was touched by her sensitivity in considering my feelings. I dug deep, thanked her for her kindness, and assured her that I would be fine if she announced her news at the dinner—and then prayed fervently that I would be. Thanks perhaps to these prayers, I managed to hold my emotions together during her announcement, and was even able to add some comments to the excited buzz that followed. I realized with hindsight that it was one of the hardest things I'd ever done.

The months passed, spring arrived, and my friend Kim planned a shower for Liz. It was to take place in mid-May—Mother's Day weekend, a holiday that, for the first time in my life, was a painful one. In fact, as May approached and the shower drew near, I felt the force of my old grief reasserting itself. My would-be due date was only a month away; its approach was a painful reminder of how different my life could have been. I became less and less sure that I could bear a celebration of someone else's pregnancy, even if it was that of a valued friend. For over a week I played ferocious games of emotional Ping-Pong: Should I go or not go? Every day—actually every hour—brought a different answer.

A few days before the event, I sent Liz an e-mail. "I'm really sorry," I told her, "but as my due date approaches, I'm feeling another wave of the old grief. If it's OK with you, I'll see how I'm feeling on the morning of the shower, and decide then whether I'm strong enough to come." She sent back a lovely and sympathetic response—"Feel free to do whatever you need to," she told me. "I completely understand."

The morning of the shower itself, I pottered around the house in a maze of indecision. *You should be bigger than your grief and—let's be honest here—you're envious,* said one voice. *On the other hand,* an equally persuasive voice chimed in, *what if you go and you are miserable and make everyone else miserable? Isn't that worse than not going?* Desperate for clarity, I said some prayers in the direction of the folk art Mary statue in my living room. I'd put some yellow backyard roses next to her, in a green vase, a kind of May altar. I waited hopefully for a sign. Nothing happened.

At a loss, I switched on the TV. PBS was showing the last ten minutes of a program about, of all subjects, Lourdes. I snapped to attention. The bearded host was talking about the miracles that had taken place there, so many of them, defying all medical explanation. "Many people believe that miracles bring faith," he mused. "In fact, it's more correct to say the opposite. It's faith that brings miracles."

He seemed to be speaking directly to me. After all, what was my struggle but a fundamental lack of faith? At its core that was the issue: the fear that Liz would have a baby and I never would, that I would never have my own chance to celebrate an upcoming birth. I believed, in some deep secret part of myself, that there were only so many pieces of the pie, and that if someone else got a wedge, I'd forever be hungry. It was irrational, and I knew it, but I couldn't quite jettison those deeply rooted feelings.

Still in my pajamas, I grabbed my rosary and headed outside. When my own thought processes fail me, the meditative repetition of the rosary has the power to break me out of my mental deadlock. Sitting in a patio chair under a foggy morning sky, I began to pray the Joyful Mysteries.

It was when I got to the second mystery that clarity suddenly broke through the haze. For the first time, I understood the essence of the Visitation: It was a story about one woman supporting another. There on the patio, I reflected on Mary and Elizabeth, each on her own journey, coming together to honor the other's joy and fear. I played with the rosary beads, praying and thinking. Through her sensitivity and awareness, Liz had certainly honored my experience. Could I honor hers? Could I be community for her at this exciting time of her life? Could I, for once, lead with friendship and Lourdes-type faith rather than with fear?

There was only one answer to that question. Three hours later I was walking into my friend Kim's backyard—somewhat tentatively, I must admit, still second-guessing my decision. But when Liz saw me, she gave me a broad smile. There in the sun we embraced each other: two women, one who was pregnant and one who was pregnant no longer, honoring each other's journey.

* * *

As so many women have discovered, the Visitation story is a beautiful example of what it means to live an active faith. It reminds us that we're all called to reach out to others, to be present in their struggles and joys. Sometimes this means traveling a physical distance; other times it requires navigating the rocky terrain of our own emotions. Either way, the Visitation proves that even the most difficult journey is worth it, for in each other's embrace we're more than the sum of our parts; we are a community, the very core of the Christian faith. Best of all, when we come together we're giving life to Mary's own son, who is born again in our encounters. "For where two or three are gathered in my name," he once promised us, "I am there among them" (Matthew 18:20).

| NATIVITY: HAVING A MOTHER, BEING A MOTHER |

In those days a decree went out from Emperor Augustus that all the world should be registered. This was the first registration and was taken while Quirinius was governor of Syria. All went to their own towns to be registered. Joseph also went from the town of Nazareth in Galilee to Judea, to the city of David called Bethlehem, because he was descended from the house and family of David. He went to be registered with Mary, to whom he was engaged and who was expecting a child. While they were there, the time came for her to deliver her child. And she gave birth to her firstborn son and wrapped him in bands of cloth, and laid him in a manger, because there was no room for them in the inn. (Luke 2:1-7)

When I was a child, my mother had a no-fail remedy for anything that was worrying me. Whether I was troubled by a nightmare, brooding over a problem at school, or haunted by a scary story I'd heard on the news, I'd find her and tell her that something was on my mind. Immediately she'd stop whatever she was doing—making dinner, folding laundry—and say, "Let's have a rock talk."

Off we'd go to the living room, where she'd sit in the wooden rocking chair and I'd curl up on her lap. As she rocked us back and forth, I'd spill out my fear while she listened, her arms around me. Within minutes, my worried little mind would unclench itself. Putting my fear into words was soothing, the motion of the chair was soothing, but above all, the close listening presence of my mother would loosen the grip of my most tenacious worries. She always knew exactly what to say to put my situation into perspective and to shrink my gargantuan fear down to an insignificant size. There was no problem bigger than my mother's ability to comfort.

Though it's been years since my last "rock talk," I've never forgotten the safety that I felt in those quiet moments. It's the same safety that I see reflected in images of Mary holding the child Jesus. Among the countless depictions of Madonna and Child that I've seen throughout my life, one of my favorites is the statue in my childhood church. It's made of light-colored wood and painted in soft pink and blue, baby colors, the shades of sunrise and sky. In this statue Mary holds Jesus near to her heart. She is looking down at him with gentle absorption and a gaze that promises the same unwavering protection that I found in my own mother. Mary and Jesus may not have had "rock talks," but there's no doubt that he grew up feeling safe and loved, always aware that his mother was a soft place for him to fall. Even the Son of God must have needed his mommy sometimes.

Many of the women I interviewed expressed a feeling of comfort with the image of Mary as a mother. Their own experiences of maternal support make it easy for them to see her as a nurturing presence, one who, like their own mothers, is always ready to listen and to soothe. Mary may be known as Our Lady of many things, but to these women, such titles are superfluous. To them, she is simply Mom.

"My mother has always been there for me, and so has Mary," says Lorelei, a thirty-four-year-old photographer. In fact, her devotion to Mary is directly due to maternal example. As a child in the Philippines, Lorelei regularly prayed the rosary with her mother and sister before the household shrine of the Holy Family. She also remembers a pilgrimage she took at age ten, when she and her mother walked to a Mary grotto: "I remember walking endlessly, being half asleep." Taxing though that experience was, Lorelei's experience of Mary has always been one of comfort, of a mother who is only a prayer away. "The first thing I always turned to was the rosary when I was depressed, had broken up with someone, or was upset about something," she says. Although her growing closeness to Jesus has recently caused Mary to fade into the background, the sense of unconditional love that the Blessed Mother evokes is still powerfully present in her spiritual life. "I've always had a sense of assurance that she's there, just being motherly and caring for me," she reflects. "My mom has always been there—she didn't approve of half of the stuff I did, but she's always been supportive no matter what. I guess you could say Mary is a reflection of my mom and vice versa."

Lisa, a thirty-four-year-old designer, also identifies Mary with her own mother. In her case, it was a connection that took many years to develop. As a child growing up in New Mexico, she was confused by references to the two Marys—Mary the Mother of God and Mary Magdalene—and thought they were the same person. Even when that misunderstanding was cleared up, the Blessed Mother always felt rather remote. "I could not feel close to her—like I knew her—the way I did with Jesus," Lisa recalls. "I wanted to know her. I really did. I just did not know how." This desire came in large part from having witnessed her own mother's close relationship with Mary. "I looked back and remembered my mom calling on our Holy Mother, *'Ay, Virgen Maria, ilumina me!'* (Oh, Virgin Mary, enlighten me!) She called on Mary during major trials, and she called on Mary in order to find the car keys." Lisa recalls that Mary not only directed her mother to the missing keys, she also led the family through more grave struggles: "Though serious illnesses had knocked on the door of our home more than once…they never stayed for dinner. I watched my mother's faith in Mary and I knew there was something to it. I knew Mom had been blessed, and through her, I was blessed."

At age twenty-eight, living and working in San Francisco, Lisa became serious about rejuvenating her spiritual life. "I cut hours at work and went on a quest to relearn/relive my faith. I fell in love with Catholicism and my Jesus all over again…and my questions about Mary resurfaced." Inspired by a supportive church community, Lisa embarked on a journey to understand God's mother more intimately. She began to pray the rosary daily, and, when asked to do a brief presentation about Mary at church, she did not let her own questions stop her. "I knew it was God's plan," she says.

In reflecting on Mary, Lisa found herself thinking about the protection and love she had always received from her own mother. "I thought about how, from one hundred miles away, my mother still reminded my twenty-eight-year-old self to brush my teeth, wear a coat and not to become an alcoholic as a result of living near the wine country," she laughs. "Then I thought of Mary, Jesus' mommy. I thought about how she had to stand back and watch as her baby was verbally degraded, beaten and put to a horrible death. I knew my own mom would give her life for me, and I imagined that Mary probably wanted to as well as she mourned for her son." It was an epiphany that made Mary real in a way that nothing else had ever done. "Suddenly, I knew her," Lisa recalls. "She was no longer a Bible character, or an impersonal deity. She was my mother."

* * *

For Lorelei and Lisa love is the thread uniting Mary and their own moms. Some of the women I interviewed, however, grew up with mothers who were distant, uninvolved or lacking in affection. As a result, the nurturing side of Mary is something they associate not with their biological mothers, but with other female figures in their lives. Two of these women described how grandmothers stepped in where their birth mothers couldn't, offering a maternal encouragement that mirrors the love of Mary herself.

Another Lisa, a thirty-nine-year-old educator and mother of three, finds that it is still painful to reflect on certain aspects of her childhood. "I grew up in an abusive home where my own mother wasn't able to accept, love and nurture me," she explains. "Despite this contentious relationship I was fortunate enough to have people in my life that loved and supported me unconditionally, my father and grandmother in particular. My grandmother, Helen, became my mother figure." As a child, Lisa found that Mary herself offered the kind of love and protection that she found in her grandmother. The statue of Mary that stood in Lisa's school corridor always gave her the sense of being cherished. "Each time I would glance at that serene face I would find comfort," she recalls. "I loved that our society would honor mothers, especially this holy one. I would leave the statue feeling stronger, even loved."

Throughout Lisa's life, prayers to Mary have always brought her peace. Today, the Memorare prayer is the equivalent of her own "rock talk," guiding her through the occasional restless night. "No matter how worried, angry, or upset I am, at some point this prayer request 'kicks in' and I feel Mary's presence with me." Through all of these experiences, Lisa has come to see Mary as the ultimate universal mother, one who is able to kiss her children's past hurts and make them better. "I believe her unconditional love helps heal these childhood wounds, making us better wives, mothers and friends," she says. "I believe that this in some small way makes the world a better place."

Like Lisa, Solange, thirty-six, grew up with a closer connection to her grandmother than to her own mother. The academic budget analyst was raised in Berkeley, California, where her father had moved to escape his "hopelessly bourgeois, conventional Catholic-school upbringing." Her parents gave her little in the way of spiritual grounding; she recalls that she "was taught to believe in sensible shoes, high-quality chocolate, fancy cheese, a healthy mistrust of authority and not much else." Her grandparents, though, were devout Irish Catholics, and Solange was exposed to their faith during the summers she spent with them. Her grandmother Dottie had lost her own mother at age thirteen, and Solange speculates that this was one reason for her grandmother's staunch devotion to Mary. Solange could relate to the feeling of being orphaned. "Like many Generation-X children, I was forced to raise myself while my parents lived a prolonged and apparently indefinite childhood and worked on 'finding themselves,'" she explains. "My grandmother was the closest thing I ever came to knowing unconditional, fully present maternal love." In fact, throughout Solange's turbulent childhood and adolescence and her "riotous" early twenties, Dottie turned to Mary in prayer, asking for protection for her granddaughter. She later told Solange that during those years, she would park by the ocean twice weekly and pray to Mary to keep her granddaughter safe. "I firmly believe that my grandmother Dottie's prayers did keep me safe in the midst of what could have been unimaginable harm," says Solange. She found her grandmother's prayers "deeply touching." Though she could not relate to Jesus, she always had a positive impression of Mary. "She was benign, maternal, oceanic," she recalls.

As Solange became an adult and her political consciousness began to take shape, she developed an aversion to Christianity. To her, the faith seemed to represent all that was repressive and wrong with a male-centered society. "The legacy of patriarchy gave women of my generation a markedly bad hangover, so I was still terribly uneasy with a Father-God and his Son," she says. Within her social milieu, however, goddess worship and a belief in the feminine divine were widely accepted, and so her affection for Mary did not seem at odds with her dislike for Christianity. During this time she found herself gathering images of Mary wherever she could find them: at dime stores, at flea markets. "Suddenly, she was in every room of my house, along with crosses, which I had slowly and almost imperceptibly started to collect."

At age thirty, Solange married a Catholic man from Ireland. Though the marriage was, as Solange recalls, "brief, beautiful and tragic," it did have a lasting and rather surprising impact on her spiritual life. She began to feel a strong pull to enter the Catholic church. A variety of complications delayed her entrance into the Rite of Christian Initiation of Adults (RCIA), but in the fall of 2005 she began the process of her adult catechism.

Entering the program, Solange felt torn, wondering how she could become Catholic when she had so many personal struggles with core aspects of the faith. "I made an inventory of my conscience when I began RCIA and asked myself how I could legitimately want to be a Catholic when I had so much trouble accepting and understanding Jesus. My heart came to rest at this: that it would take time, but that I had been hearing a call for too long to dismiss it as a passing fancy, that I already understood and accepted Mary, and that she would take me where I needed to go."

Solange decided that she would just "fake it till she made it," and stayed in the program.

Over the coming months, Solange found that Mary was indeed leading her to her Son, introducing a Jesus who was far from the repressive figure Solange had always envisioned. "I heard nothing but a message of love—God as love and Jesus as a champion of ultimate love," she explains. "I began to let go of holding Mary's hand so tightly and move toward her Son, whom I have come to understand—and I am only at the beginning of getting to know him—as a hero, a speaker of truth, one who would not tolerate the smallness of humanity, who called us to truly be God's children, in his image." Much to her surprise, she has even found joy in some of the church's dogmas and positions, a turn of events that she had never expected. She entered the church at the Easter Vigil in 2006.

Though Solange acknowledges that certain Protestant strains are more in line with her political views, to her the Catholic church has something that most other Christian religions don't: deep reverence for Mary, the mother who played such a crucial role in nurturing her own spiritual growth. "We cannot underestimate the importance of Mary to women, particularly young women, who are forming their faith," she says. "I still say a Hail Mary with my Our Fathers. I always sit on the side of the church nearest any image of Mary." To Solange, Mary is the beloved maternal figure who, like her own grandmother, never gave up on her during the turbulent times. "She is still my ultimate mother, the supreme example of patience."

* * *

These stories demonstrate the appeal Mary can hold for women who lack a close relationship with their mothers. To many of them she's a source of comfort, the loving guardian who will never fail them. For other women, though, Mary provokes an opposite reaction: Their estrangement from their own mothers is a barrier to connecting with her. Because of past wounds, some women have a hard time trusting any maternal figure, even the Blessed Mother.

It's a dynamic that Christine, an author, retreat leader and spiritual director, understands well. The forty-year-old adult convert to Catholicism found that though Jesus quickly became very present in her life, Mary was always remote. "I didn't see her as my mother—she was a distant figure whom I respected," she says. Although Christine desired to have a more personal relationship with Mary, she was at a loss to know how to make it happen. "Perhaps because I didn't have an intimately warm relationship with my mother or grandmother, I didn't know how to have that kind of relationship with my heavenly mother," she says. In fact, Christine's rocky relationship with her own mom had another impact on her life: Even though she was in a loving marriage, she was afraid to have children of her own. It was a fear that she later learned probably came from, what she calls, "some mother wound that was very deep, the way my mother had treated me or some harshness." Regardless of where the wound came from, Christine says, "I didn't trust myself to be a mother."

This began to shift on a retreat to Mali Losinj, an island near Medjugorje, in 2003. There, Christine knelt before the Blessed Sacrament, with a priest praying over her, and gave her life to Jesus. Sitting back down, she felt the Holy Spirit flood over her, and she sobbed openly, "knowing something was being healed, but not knowing what. I sensed Mary's presence near me, wanting to comfort me, on my right-hand side, and I sensed her communicating the words, asking, 'Can I put my arm around you?'" Christine recalls that she answered, "No, I don't trust you. You might hurt me." Though Christine suspected that her response was more about deeply rooted pain with her own mother than it was about Mary, she still couldn't get past her feelings of suspicion. She explains, "The little girl in me knew she simply didn't trust this woman near her. But as I sobbed further, I let her come closer, and I said, 'You can just touch my hand.' As I sobbed further, I sensed her envelop me more and more. That whole experience was a healing of something from my past." It was only a day or two later that Christine realized what the healing was:

She was no longer frightened by the thought of being a mother. Her old fear of having children never returned.

Though this incident represented progress in Christine's relationship with Mary, it was still difficult to break completely out of the old cycle of suspicion. "There was still that child in me that said, 'I don't quite trust you,'" she recalls. Months later, though, one of Christine's counselees, a woman with the gift of prophecy, gave Christine a surprising message. "One day, she said she saw that my heart would receive a dark jab, a dark piercing jab, and then I'd know Mary's love like I never had before." The message was worrisome to Christine, who had severe arrhythmia, a heart condition. When she pressed the woman for more information, the woman assured her that her physical health would be fine; it was an emotional jab that Christine would experience. Christine puzzled over the message for a few days, then let it rest.

Soon after this conversation, Christine was scheduled to have an ablation, a medical procedure to correct her rapid heartbeats. Understandably, she was frightened by the procedure, which involved inserting an electrode into her heart. It was a time when she craved a mother's support, but such encouragement was not forthcoming. "My parents and aunt came over for dinner the night before the procedure—my mother seemed to be acting a bit cold toward me," she recalls. "Nothing was said about my procedure." The ablation went well, and the next day, Christine was flooded with calls from the important people in her life—all but one. "Everyone, even acquaintances, called me the next day to make sure I was OK, but not my mother, and then she didn't call the next day." Finally, Christine called her mother to ask why she hadn't checked in about her daughter's health. Christine recalls her mother's explanation: "She said she was too busy at work. The rest of my family thought nothing of it. I was crushed."

Deeply upset, Christine called a friend and described her mother's coldness. "Does she even care?" she wondered aloud. "Then, as I was crying, my friend said, 'I sense Mary, she's here, she's here—I feel her presence so strongly. She's waited for this moment all your life. She's been there for you ever since you were a little girl. She wants you to let her into your heart and she's telling me that now you're finally able to feel her.'" For the first time, Christine felt that she could completely open herself to Mary's love. "I could barely speak, I just wanted to cry. That was the first time I'd accepted her full embrace and accepted her as my mother, knowing that she was the only mother I had who could truly comfort me."

Shortly after this experience, Christine attended a conference on Medjugorje. On a large screen was projected an image of Mary, and as Christine looked at it, she felt how far she had come in accepting Mary as her spiritual mother. As Christine stared at her, she recalls, "I felt her staring back, and I felt her love pierce my heart as the song played in the background: 'Long have I waited for your coming home to me and living deeply our new life.'"[1] For Christine, there was no doubt as to where the song was coming from, or for whom it was intended. "She was singing right to me."

* * *

One of the most beautiful aspects of Mary's role as the Mother of Jesus is that it provides a changing way for women to connect with her. Although many women, particularly younger ones, identify with the child held safe in Mary's arms, my interviews have shown that when women become mothers, they often grow into a feeling of kinship with Mary herself. For these women, Mary is a confidante and a source of wisdom, one who understands the all-consuming experience of helping a little one grow into adulthood.

MaryJo, a fifty-five-year-old first grade teacher at a parochial school, describes how her image of Mary has changed as she has grown up and raised a family of her own. In her earlier years, she always adored Mary, who was a source of maternal comfort. "As a young child, I had nightmares," she recalls. "My mother bought me a glow-in-the-dark rosary to place under my pillow during the night. I would hold onto it and fall asleep praying it." That was the end of MaryJo's nightmares, and the beginning of a lifelong ritual: "To this day, my rosary is beside me each night and I often fall asleep praying it."

As MaryJo grew up, she found that her experience of Mary became more layered and complex. "I think it was in my twenties when my view of Mary changed from an image of a shy and humble girl to a strong and determined woman," she recalls. It's an image of the Blessed Mother that continues to be shaped by MaryJo's own experiences of family life; she has raised three children, now adults, and suffered the loss of her husband Bill to cancer. She reflects on her relationship with Mary and how it has grown over the course of several years: "I think as I have aged as a woman and mother, I have come to understand the challenges Mary faced as she aged. As I meet life's challenges, I think of the frustration she must have felt, yet always presented an image of patience. Once children are grown, they continue to bring heartache (usually unintentionally) to a parent. Having a husband suffer and die, a son enlist in the army after 9/11, and another son and daughter with health issues, have just reinforced for me that women are the backbones and source of strength in many families. This must have been true with Mary." In the Blessed Mother, MaryJo has found a personal model for how to live the ever-evolving vocation of motherhood, a calling that doesn't end when the children leave the nest.

Though her own children are much younger, Trish, thirty-nine, a law school instructor and mother of two, has also found strength in the image of Mary as a mother. Unlike MaryJo, Trish's affection for the Blessed Mother began as an adult. In her younger years, Trish remembers fondly being "very much into stories," so she always felt a strong connection to Jesus, who she remembers as "the fascinating parable-teller." For Trish, Jesus' mother, on the other hand, was always far less compelling. "With Mary, the comparative dearth of stories contributed to an incomplete and unintriguing picture," she says.

In 1998, though, on a trip to the Holy Land, Trish was walking one afternoon not far from Cana. At that moment, she had an epiphany: "I had a moment of startling 'heart knowledge' as the late afternoon sun lit up a hill of olive trees that God had come here, to this earth, to be one of us." Though she had always known this on an intellectual level, she had never truly felt its impact until that moment. "This God of ours did not descend from heaven to visit in a royal spaceship. This God became one of us, lived with us, befriended us, loved us," she explains. She soon found that this new understanding of the Incarnation also enriched her image of Mary; just as Jesus became more fleshed out, so too did the woman who had agreed to carry him in her womb.

When Trish herself became a mother, her understanding of Mary became even more personal. "Unlike men, women are capable of having this cellular experience of bearing another life within them, of being 'cocreators' with the divine, of being a vehicle through which God fashions a perfect, unique and awesome little soul," she reflects. She goes on to say, "From the moment a woman learns about the tiny child within her, she has a supernatural instinct to protect, nurture and love her child. And yet she knows that the child is not really 'hers' and that she is just the instrument through which this wholly other person comes into being." Along with maternal joy, though, comes the possibility of all kinds of heartache, Trish acknowledges, "the devastating suffering that accompanies any kind of pregnancy loss, the death of a child and even the paralyzing fear of that loss, which can overwhelm you with no warning. Because Mary was a human being, a real woman, a mother and a mother who suffered the ultimate loss, she does understand all of this—and a woman can go to her and pour it out to her." On the journey of motherhood, Trish has found Mary to be a source not just of emotional encouragement, but of physical support as well. "I had a moment during childbirth which was more difficult than I had anticipated," she recalls. "I really found myself meditating on—almost leaning on—Mary's presence and strength to get through the moment."

Even the daily frustrations of motherhood, Trish has learned, can be brought to the feet of the Blessed Mother. She describes a recent day of near-despair: "I felt quite overwhelmed by my two small children and the never-ending tasks and I had lost my patience and snapped at my toddler."

Later, attending Mass, she found herself weeping on the way back from the Communion line. "I walked straight outside and found myself at Mary's grotto. As I stood there and just sobbed, I prayed with Mary to help me be a good mom to those beautiful children who are so perfect and so much better than anything I could have 'earned' or deserved," she explains. She recalls, "I abruptly stopped sobbing when I saw Mary's bare feet—just like when my baby girl stops crying when I pick her up. There was that simple reminder that she was one of us, she understands. She walked here on this earth, she loved her child desperately, she said 'yes' to God even though she had no idea what the implications were for her or for the rest of us."

For Trish, that reminder of Mary as a human mother was exactly what she needed: "It gave me strength and comfort, as it has given so many women." In Mary's example, she continues to find the recipe for how to make it through the many challenges of parenting. "I will love these children, I will be bold enough to ask for the gifts I need to bring God's love to them and others," she explains. "I will try not to fear loss and I will try to echo Mary's brave 'yes.'"

* * *

Any woman who has ever been pregnant, given birth or cared for a baby knows how physical the act of mothering is. For all its emotional power, there's a fundamental concreteness, an earthiness to the vocation of being a mom. At the same time, though, there's a kind of mothering that is more symbolic than physical. Maria, a graduate student in theology, calls it "spiritual mothering." As she explains, it's a way that childless women can relate personally to Mary's maternity.

Maria first became interested in this topic during a course on the Bible in the arts, when she wrote a paper about how the image of the pregnant Mary has been depicted throughout the centuries. A classmate suggested that she consider what this pregnant Mary means to those who are childless. Intrigued, Maria found herself pondering that very question: "What can the pregnant Mary mean to each of us—whether we are men or women, single or married, don't or can't have children?" she wondered.

First of all, she realized that it requires a more nuanced understanding of Mary's maternal role. "When we think of Mary, we think of her first and foremost as the physical mother of Jesus," she acknowledges. "However, Jesus himself teaches that each one of us can become his mother. We become his mother in two ways: by hearing the Word of God and by acting on it. In other words, we become his mother through our faith and good works." Maria explains that this commitment to Christ's message affects the way that we interact with those around us. "Through our faith and works, we in turn can exercise a maternal charity toward others," she says. "Spiritual motherhood includes nurturing the social, moral, emotional, cultural and spiritual lives of others. When we pray daily and build community with others, we become spiritual parents." It's a role that is beautifully universal. "We can be spiritual parents anywhere—in the office, at the grocery store, on the bus, in the classroom, with our nephews and nieces, with our parish youth group, on the phone," she explains. In fact, those who do not have their own children to care for are often freer to exercise this motherhood than others: "Being childless can motivate us to move outside of ourselves and to give ourselves in charity to those around us. It can give us greater freedom to pursue and accomplish the unique work that God calls each of us to do."

In the end, Maria understands that motherhood is not simply a biological reality; it's a calling that can be lived every day, everywhere, with everyone we encounter. "The pregnant Mary, our spiritual mother, can inspire us to conceive Christ in faith and obedience, and to bring him into the world again as we reach out in love to others," she muses. "We can mirror her spiritual maternity by welcoming as our own children those whom Jesus has invited into our lives."

* * *

It's easy to see why the image of Mary as mother is such a beloved one, transcending cultures and centuries. Many of us identify with the figure of a mother holding her child, offering him a safe haven from the terrors of the world outside. In Mary and Jesus' case, it's a terror that was all too real; persecution, humiliation, torture and death crouched just outside the circle of her arms. But I like to think that those quiet mother-and-son moments strengthened the adult Jesus to face the challenges of his ministry, helping him recognize that some things are larger than hate and pain. In her own way, Mary too must have found a deep joy in nurturing her Son into his unique calling. Certainly, if these women's stories are any indication, the Madonna and Child resonate with us because they remind us of all that is good in human relationships. Whether we identify with the mother who gives love or the child who receives it, the figure of Mary and Jesus together taps into our most basic human desires: to love and to be loved, unconditionally.

| OUR LADY OF SORROWS: GRIEVING LOSSES |

And the child's father and mother were amazed at what was being said about him. Then Simeon blessed them and said to his mother Mary, "This child is destined for the falling and the rising of many in Israel, and to be a sign that will be opposed so that the inner thoughts of many may be revealed—and a sword will pierce your own soul, too." (Luke 2:33-35)

Many traditional depictions of Mary show her pointing to her heart, a visible heart that is crowned with flame and pierced by swords. It's a familiar image, one that I've seen thousands of times throughout my Catholic life. These pictures are usually so beautiful, with their pastel colors and Mary's lovely face, that it comes as a shock to think about what they represent: a woman whose heart is gravely wounded, under attack by both fire and iron.

The classic image of the Pietà shows us the reason for Mary's pain. In it, we see a mother cradling her Son's body, a gesture that recalls the happier moments when she held her infant Son close to her heart. This time, though, the life in him has gone, and so too has a part of herself, as she lives a nightmare that no parent should have to endure. One of the side altars of my church features a large statue of this scene. Jesus' limbs trail on the ground and Mary's eyes are raised to heaven, as if struggling to find some reason for the brutality of her Son's death. On the woodwork above the statue is carved a line from Lamentations: *Attend and see if there be any sorrows like to my sorrows.*

There was a point in my life when images such as these—the pierced heart, the sorrowful mother—were foreign to me. They seemed maudlin and excessive, a relic from some medieval era of Catholicism, where

suffering was glorified. At that time, I was critical of what I saw as the neg-
ativity of traditional Catholicism, and such images seemed downright
unhealthy. *Why keep emphasizing the suffering?* I'd ask myself. *There's
enough loss in the world; why can't church be a refuge, a place to escape from
thoughts of pain?*

At that time, I hadn't yet learned an essential human truth: The best
way to heal from pain is not to run from it, but rather to acknowledge its
existence. I hadn't yet learned that in moments of loss, there is no comfort
quite like being in the presence of someone who will listen as we pour out
our grief. The truth is that when we are most vulnerable, we don't need
empty platitudes and false cheer. We need the quiet sympathy of one who
has been there before, a friend who knows exactly what it feels like to be
caught in the fierce grip of unimaginable pain.

In other words, we need someone like Our Lady of Sorrows.

* * *

Simeon's words apply to us all: At some point, each one of us will have a
heart pierced by loss. When we open ourselves up to life, we also invite the
possibility of pain. Relationships come to an end, loved ones die, lifestyles
have to be modified in the face of age or illness, deeply cherished hopes
never materialize. Thanks to Christ's Resurrection, we know that earthly
suffering is not the end of the story; nonetheless, for those who live in the
midst of any kind of anguish, the long view can be very hard to embrace.
It's during these trying times that we wonder whether there really is any
other sorrow like our sorrow.

For some of the women I interviewed, the fact that Mary has experienced intense grief makes her a very accessible figure. She's not the superficial friend you call only when everything is going well, but the woman
who understands your pain, and who lends support at your most vulnerable moments. Sandra, a thirty-two-year-old investment consultant, has
certainly discovered the power of Mary's comfort. "The times when I've
identified with Mary the most are when I've come across a difficult situation, primarily in the love department," she explains. It's noteworthy

because Mary is usually not Sandra's preferred intercessor; in fact, the Blessed Mother has traditionally been a minor figure in her prayer life. "I see this hierarchical order," she explains. "I see God at the very top, then I see Jesus and then I see Mary along with the saints. For the longest time I have either gone to God or to the saints to intercede on my behalf, but I usually skip right over Jesus and Mary."

Recently, though, Sandra found herself leaning on Mary in a moment of emotional anxiety, an episode that followed the breakup of a romantic relationship. "I'd just gotten into my car in my old neighborhood; my former boyfriend still lives in the area," she explains. "I saw a car very similar to his pull into the parking lot." The sight of it resurrected the many painful emotions that had followed the ending of their relationship. "I thought, 'Oh, God, I hope that's not him, I just don't want to see him right now, especially if he's already with a significant other.'" Fidgeting in the driver's seat, Sandra did something she never does—she hit the AM button on her radio. On the air came a Catholic station that was broadcasting the rosary. She was instantly aware of Mary's presence. "It was this huge, powerful, literally bringing-me-to-tears-type of thing," she recalls. As she sat there and watched the car park in the distance, she prayed, "Mary, help me, help me, help me get through this experience because I can't handle this right now. This is just too difficult for me; give me the strength that you had to get through your difficult challenges." Though Sandra knew that her own pain was minor compared to what Mary had suffered, she felt the power of praying to a woman who understood what it was like to be in the clutches of severe grief. "Even as I left that parking lot, I was still praying to her—I told her, 'You know, I still need to move on from this relationship. I need your help. I need your intercession. I need to be as strong as you were, as you are.'" It was a shift in Sandra's view of Mary. "At that point I found myself relating to her for maybe the first time ever, really, and seeing her as another female to help me."

Reflecting on this, Sandra admits that she feels a sense of guilt that she only turns to Mary when she is in pain. At the same time, it's a response that makes perfect sense to her. Mary's female nature, paired with the tragedy she endured, makes her a truly relatable figure. "While there are female saints that I pray to, I think that the loss of her Son, the way she lost him...I can't imagine a more intense pain than she must have gone through," she reflects. It's an understanding of Mary that helps put everything in Sandra's life into perspective. "She's someone who has gone through the ultimate form of pain, so I feel like, 'Can you help me with my teeny, tiny pain, because you've been there, you've been through a lot greater—help me with my insignificant pain.'"

Sandra isn't the only one who has found that suffering can lead to a new understanding of Jesus' mother. Rosemary, a fifty-eight-year-old executive assistant, describes a childhood in which Mary was always there: Her mother had a statue of Mary on the bedroom dresser, Rosemary attended May crownings and the Blessed Mother was the namesake for most of the women in the family. "Both of my grandmothers were named Mary, my mother was named Mary and I am named Rosemary," she explains. "If your name wasn't Mary, it was your middle name," she laughs. Rosemary grew up with what recalls as "a warm feeling about Mary," but it wasn't until recently that her understanding of the Blessed Mother went to a deeper level. This shift was inspired in part by the film *The Passion of the Christ*, a movie that Rosemary had approached with a specific set of expectations. "I thought I would learn more about Christ by feeling what he felt," she says. "To my surprise, I felt what Mary felt. This beautiful idealized statue became a real woman. She was dressed in drab clothes, not so pretty and not so peaceful."

The suffering of Jesus' mother evokes another loss, one that Rosemary witnessed decades ago. "When I was first married and had a young child, my husband's aunt lost her twenty-one-year-old son in a car accident," she explains. It devastated the young man's mother. "All I can remember was walking into the funeral home and seeing the grief on her face. She was no longer the person I knew. There was a hollowness in her eyes and a lack of life in her face. She had died, too. Even a year after the funeral, she looked the same," says Rosemary. Decades later, Rosemary still remembers that lifeless expression, a mother's grief, which she now relates to Mary. "Thoughts of Mary did not come to me at that time, but now when I hear the Passion, I can see Mary's pain of the suffering and loss of her son, as I again see the face of the aunt so long ago," she explains.

Rosemary's story shows that though the average life is made up of millions of neutral to happy moments, it's the painful experiences that often become the most indelible markers on the journey. These moments of suffering are reminders of a reality that we tend to forget: the fragility of life, and how quickly and unexpectedly it can be taken away. Naturally, it's a lesson that holds a particular terror for parents. Maria, thirty-four, has learned firsthand that seeing one's own child in danger can alter every-thing—even one's lifelong attitude toward Mary. "I grew up in a Catholic home, attending thirteen years of Catholic school, so I have the typical experience of saying the Hail Mary, of attending Mary crownings, of get-ting a rosary for my First Communion, of having a Mary statue in the gar-den," says the teacher turned stay-at-home mom. "None of this ever both-ered me, but it didn't click for me personally either. It was just what we did," she muses. One thing that was slightly more personal to her was having the name of the Blessed Mother. "Growing up in a Hungarian family, we celebrated our feast days, and mine was December 8, the Immaculate Conception." Maria recalls that her mother would fix the menu of her choice and her grandmother would bring doughnuts, which made it what she calls "a day worth celebrating." Nonetheless, even this yearly anniversary was not particularly meaningful, because she says, "It was always too much to live up to, and seemed a bit contrived."

Even though Jesus' mother has never been a very significant part of her life, Maria describes a recent experience that helped her see Mary in an entirely new light. It happened on a Sunday, Maria's birthday, when her daughter Charlotte was fifteen months old. Maria was hosting a book club for her friends, and recalls that her little girl was acting very whiny and clingy. Maria attributed this behavior to the fact that Charlotte had had a slight fever earlier in the day, as well as to the fact that Maria's guests were taking some of the attention away from her daughter. "I remember her hanging around me, and I took her into my lap. She was sitting there very still, which was uncharacteristic of her," Maria remembers. "At one point I looked at her and she didn't look like herself." Concerned, Maria brought Charlotte into the bedroom and showed her husband. "He took one look at her and said, 'Maria, we have to take her to the ER—her pupils are completely fixed and dilated.'" Charlotte started to shake, and it was then that they realized she was having some kind of a seizure.

Waiting for the paramedics to arrive, Maria was living a parent's nightmare: the knowledge that her child was in danger, paired with an inability to do anything to help. Charlotte's listlessness and her fixed eyes were something Maria had never seen before. "When I was holding her and looking at her and feeling like she wasn't there, I had the feeling of this is what it's like to hold a dead child," Maria remembers. When the paramedics arrived and Charlotte was being carried out to the ambulance, she came out of her seizure. Nonetheless, the paramedics took her to the hospital for hours of tests. Even in the midst of her relief, Maria felt still more pain at seeing her little girl poked and prodded by the medical team. "I had to hold her down while they were working on her," she recalls. It turned out to be a febrile seizure, the first of several that Charlotte would have over the next few years. She has since outgrown them.

At the time, Maria didn't connect the episode with Mary. The following Lent, though, she found that her experience of the season was transformed. "I remember during that Holy Week that what had struck me the most was experiencing the whole Passion from Mary's perspective," she explains. She had flashbacks to what it had felt like to hold Charlotte's limp body, and "it sort of made me feel what the pain must have been like to Mary. But she had lost her child, and I still had mine." She explains that this experience was the closest she had ever felt to Mary, and that she gained a new respect for Mary's strength: "I really saw the events from Mary's perspective and caught a glimpse of what she went through and what she sacrificed to be the mother of Jesus."

Though Mary is loved for many things—her faith, her grace, her beauty—it's her vulnerability that makes the Blessed Mother accessible to Maria. "Personally, I think I can identify with her more and consider following her example when I think of her as someone more human than she is usually portrayed," she explains. Some people say that nothing unites like grief, and for Maria this has certainly been true: It was a shared experience of maternal pain that brought Mary, at last, to life.

* * *

Although the title Our Lady of Sorrows refers to Mary's loss of her son, Jesus' death was not her first encounter with grief. Though the Gospels are silent on the details, we know that Mary also lost her husband, Joseph. Joseph's last active role in the Gospels comes during the story of Jesus being found in the Temple, when Joseph and Mary discover their Son teaching the chief priests. At some point between that event and the beginning of Jesus' adult ministry, Mary became a widow.

The circumstances of Joseph's death are unknown to us, but there's little doubt that Mary mourned the loss of her husband. Joseph, the quiet figure in the background, had repeatedly shown the depth of his love for his small family. In many ways, one could say that his life was geared toward protection: He stood by Mary in the early days, marrying a woman who was pregnant with a child that was not his own. In a crowded city, he scouted out a private place for his wife to give birth, ensuring a roof over her head. When Herod's bloodlust threatened Joseph's family, he led them to a safe harbor in a foreign land. Though the Gospels are silent on the personal relationship between husband and wife, all of the evidence points to a generous and gentle man who made numerous sacrifices to protect his wife and child. His death must have been a great sorrow to Mary.

Alberta, sixty-two, understands the pain that comes from losing a spouse who has shared so much of one's life. In 2004 the former elementary school teacher lost her husband, Page, to cancer. In many ways, his death was the final step on a spiritual journey that they had walked together for decades. They were married in the Catholic church, but then drifted into the New Age movement. "For twenty-two years, we were away from the church," Alberta explains. It was a visit to some devout Protestant relatives that inspired Alberta and Page to return to Christianity. They came back to the church in 1993, and Page joined Alberta in becoming a secular Franciscan; he later became the minister for their fraternity. Then, in 2003, he was diagnosed with liver cancer.

When Page was ill, Alberta turned often to Mary, who seemed to have an intimate understanding of her pain. She explains, "I would just talk to Mary and say, 'I know you understand. How did you do it when Joseph was dying? You were a widow and I'm a widow. Please help me, Mary.'" She also found comfort in praying the rosary, a practice she had begun when she rejoined the church. The daily experience of caring for her dying husband was also something she brought to Mary. She recalls a time when her husband, Page, was still alive and she was caring for him. She would talk to Mary and sometimes plead, "I know you took care of Joseph and helped him. Please intercede for us so we will both have the strength spiritually and physically to do what is necessary. Did you sit up nights with Joseph? Did you bring him a drink of water? What a happy death Joseph had to be with you and Jesus at the end of his life. Please intercede with your Son for Page to have a peaceful death."

Alberta is convinced that Mary heard her pleas. On the afternoon of September 12, 2004, Page was anointed by a priest. Nearly four and a half hours later, the loved ones keeping vigil by his bed spontaneously prayed the Our Father. It's a moment that Alberta remembers vividly: "When we said, 'Amen,' we could hear a soft, long exhalation and Page very peacefully was gone. The windows were open and the birds sang and the air was warm."

Throughout her adjustment to life as a widow, Alberta has continued to find solace in Mary's presence. "I still talk to Mary and ask her for help in the loneliness and strangeness of no longer sharing my life with my spouse," she explains. Grief is a long process, healing takes time and nobody understands that better than the woman who lost both of the men she loved: her husband and her son. And just as Mary kept her faith even in the most difficult circumstances, Alberta has learned that one of the steps toward healing is learning how to integrate the loss into one's overall spiritual journey. She comments, "One thing I have learned is that the question is not, 'Why did this happen?', but 'What do you want me to learn from this, and how may I better serve you, Lord, because of this life experience?'"

* * *

One thing that distinguishes Our Lady of Sorrows from the other names given to Mary is that few of us, if asked, would choose to identify with this particular title. Most of us want a life that is full of happiness, not mourning. Although Alberta's question is a crucial one, it takes time to reach the point when we are strong enough to ponder it. When storm clouds roll in and mar the peaceful landscapes of our lives, it's not uncommon to feel resentment, even anger, at the thought of what we have lost.

I've learned firsthand how sorrow can shake a spiritual belief system to its core. Following my ectopic pregnancy in 2004, I was terrified to try to conceive again. Statistics indicated that I had a thirty percent chance of having another ectopic pregnancy; the loss had been so wrenching that I doubted whether I could handle another one. Still, I knew there was no way to have a child without taking that risk.

During the next few months, my thoughts often turned to Mary. I pictured her not as Our Lady of Sorrows but as the woman depicted in the statue on my bedroom shelf, one that I'd found at a secondhand shop shortly after we started trying to conceive. Something compelled me to buy it, and the little statue became a symbol of my hopefulness for the future. It was a peaceful, lovely Mary, painted in white and blue. In her cupped palms she cradled a pink rose, and she smiled into the depths of its petals as if taking joy in its beauty. The serenity of her face gave me hope that I, too, would one day be delighting in new life.

Two months later, on a vacation with my in-laws, I had a strong sense that I was pregnant. I wanted to be excited, but the fear of another ectopic pregnancy constricted my joy. The only thing that mitigated my anxiety was to retreat to the room Scott and I shared in the lake cottage, sit on the bed and pray the rosary. The repeated prayers and the sense of closeness to the Blessed Mother would break me out of the hamster wheel in my mind, and I'd be able to rejoin the others, temporarily at peace.

Back home, a positive pregnancy test confirmed what I already knew. Again, our excitement was tempered with fear until we went in for an ultrasound at six weeks. Scott held my hand, and I held my breath as the doctor switched off the light and the dark image of my uterus came into view. I was afraid to look at the screen. "Oh, look, there we are," said the doctor, her tone light. "Everything's fine. There's no heartbeat yet, but we're probably a day too early to be able to see that. This is definitely not an ectopic," she reassured us. We left the doctor's office giddy with excitement and relief.

In the month that followed, I felt overjoyed, truly as if a prayer had been answered. I welcomed the nausea—what did such discomfort matter? The baby was fine, and I was fine. I smiled often at Mary those days, feeling a wave of kinship between us. She'd been looking out for me, and I knew, beyond a doubt, that she was taking joy in my happiness.

At ten weeks, on September 15, we returned to the doctor for our first prenatal appointment. It felt liberating to be going in for an ultrasound without fear. We chatted lightheartedly with the nurse, who did her calculations and told us that the due date would be April 14. "Oh, that's Good Friday," Scott said. I liked the idea of an Easter baby.

When the doctor wheeled in the ultrasound machine, Scott reached for my hand, this time in shared excitement, not anxiety. The doctor flipped off the lights, and once again the black image of my uterus came into view, with a grainy white figure in the center. "Is that the baby?" I asked. "Yes," the doctor said. She was quiet for several minutes, moving the probe, hitting buttons, measuring, as I absorbed the sight of that white splotch on the screen, my little Easter baby. The only sound was the clicking of keys on the pad as she recorded the images.

Suddenly, it occurred to me that she seemed to be taking a very long time to say anything. I felt a curl of fear inside my chest. Scott and I were perfectly still, waiting for her to speak.

"OK," said the doctor at last, and her voice was careful, as if she were choosing her words with deliberation. "Let me tell you what I see." Scott's hand kneaded mine, our palms damp with fear. "There's no heartbeat, and I should be seeing a clear one at this point." She measured. "You're at ten weeks, but the baby's growth is only eight and a half weeks. Somewhere, probably in the last week or so, the baby's heart stopped beating." I couldn't say anything. It was as if the ceiling had fallen on my chest. The doctor touched my leg. "I'm so sorry," she said. "When this happens, it's usually due to a chromosomal abnormality with the fetus. It's nothing you did or didn't do." A second doctor came in to offer his opinion, and he gave the same diagnosis. "No fetal heartbeat," he said, "and at this point in pregnancy, even an untrained eye should be able to see it. I'm so sorry."

Scott and I filed out of the doctor's office mutely, numb with shock. The afternoon passed like a nightmare as we cried, broke the news to my parents, then cried some more. Only later did I realize the significance of the date. It was September 15, the feast day of Our Lady of Sorrows.

For the first time ever, I felt angry at Mary. It all seemed too neat somehow, too contrived to be a mere coincidence. The Good Friday due date took on an uncanny, horrible symbolism. Did I really believe that Mary had engineered this sad outcome, or planned it around those significant days? No, I didn't, but I felt an undeniable sense of betrayal. She was supposed to be on my side, but her intercession had not protected my baby the way that I had expected. Though I'd known that many pregnancies end in miscarriage, I'd been sure that such a tragedy could not happen to us; surely Mary's intercession would prevent a second loss. At that time I was in the early stages of researching this book, and I went about it mechanically, devoid of feeling. It was hard to feel any great enthusiasm for Mary, or for God either. Adding to the emotional pain was the fact that my body wasn't miscarrying on its own, common in such cases. It was excruciating to know that I was walking around with my dead child inside me. I felt like a living tomb.

On the day of the dilation-and-curettage (D & C) surgery to remove the dead baby, I lay on the operating table, nervous and depressed. I stared at the huge round lights above me, with a kind nurse patting my arm and watching me intently to gauge the effects of the anesthesia. In spite of my distance from Mary, I found that the only prayer that I could say was the Hail, Holy Queen. "To you do we send up our sighs, mourning and weeping in this valley of tears," I thought, as the aqua-suited doctors and nurses moved about, preparing for a procedure I'd never expected to have. I continued to pray, "Turn then, O most gracious advocate, your eyes of mercy toward us...." It soothed me, there in my own valley of tears, to drift off to unconsciousness in the middle of that prayer. Even in my own pain, I knew that I was speaking to a woman who understood mourning and weeping.

Looking back now, I see that as the beginning of my softening toward Mary. There wasn't a magical moment of epiphany in which I moved past my disappointment in her; it was a gradual process, happening in barely perceptible steps, just like the healing itself. During the months following my surgery, I found a huge comfort in talking to other women who had miscarried. There were a great many of them, even among my own circle of friends. Nothing helped quite like sharing my story and hearing how they had healed from their own losses. Against this background, my feelings toward Mary shifted gradually, moving from anger to a sense of kinship. I didn't know why we had lost the baby, but I learned to rest in that mystery and to focus instead on the connection between her loss and mine. She became one more face in the support group of women that I had gathered around me.

I also gained a new perspective on the suffering of women, like Mary, who had given birth to their children only to lose them years later. News reports of toddlers or teenagers killed in accidents moved me to tears as I thought about the mothers who had raised them, who had known and loved their children in a way that I hadn't had time to do. I recognized that my own loss couldn't come close, but for the first time, I felt that I had some small inkling of the monumental grief that they endured. Similarly, when I thought of Mary, I had a new perspective on what it must have been like to see her thirty-three-year-old Son nailed to a cross, far out of reach, dying slowly in the sun. How she endured it I did not know, and I still don't. I only know that these musings gradually led me to the moment when I could think of our shared feast day with sympathy for what she had suffered, not resentment at my own loss. A sword had pierced her heart, one had pierced mine, too, and in the awareness of those shared wounds, we were reunited. She had always been my friend; at last, once again, I was hers.

* * *

In moments of grief, it's hard to be in the company of someone who has had what we deem a painless life. They seem to us to have no hard-won wisdom or empathy with which to comfort us. In Mary, though, we find the opposite: a woman who walks with familiarity into the middle of our worst suffering. While many people find solace in seeing her as a powerful figure, one whose intercession can lessen our pain, sometimes there's a more visceral comfort in remembering her vulnerability. When we're lost in our own pain, walking that lonely road between death and resurrection, we meet the distraught mother by the wayside and find that she is just like us: a woman whose grief is surpassed only by her love.

| OUR HEAVENLY INTERCESSOR: PRAYING WITH MARY |

To pray to Our Lady means not to substitute her for Christ, but to glorify her Son who desires us to have loving confidence in His Saints, especially in His Mother.

— "Behold Your Mother: Woman of Faith," National Conference of Catholic Bishops[1]

Years ago, while living in France, I visited countless churches—everything from vast cavernous cathedrals to modest country chapels. Nearly every one of them had a wall decorated with small marble plaques. These plaques were engraved with the statement *Reconnaissance à Marie*, which translated means "Gratitude to Mary" or more loosely translated, "Give Thanks to Mary." Often there were initials or a name at the bottom, along with a date from the nineteenth or early twentieth century.

Those plaques fascinated me. Clearly, each one told a story of faith: Someone had prayed to Mary for intercession, the prayers had been answered, and the grateful party had put up a tangible, lasting witness to her power. Sadly, there's no way to learn the stories behind the prayers. Looking at any given plaque, I can only speculate as to whether an illness was cured, a relationship healed, or a farm saved from ruin. Still, one thing is clear: For centuries, people have come to Mary with their most personal and pressing needs.

Prayers to Mary are often misunderstood, both inside and outside of the church. Many are suspicious of those who seem to elevate her power, or put her on a level with God. The church, though, is clear that Christ alone is the source of grace. When we pray to Mary or to the saints, we are asking them to add their prayers to ours, much as we would ask a good friend to pray for us. In the tradition of the church, Mary is viewed as a particularly powerful intercessor, not only because she played a critical role in salvation history but because of her unique relationship to Christ. As many Catholics like to say, when a loving mother asks a favor of her devoted son, how can he refuse?

Given this tradition, it's no surprise that many women remember Marian prayers as being among the first they ever learned. Mary Ann, a sixty-year-old registered nurse, remembers the spirituality of her grandmother from Lebanon. She recalls, "She was educated in convents and had a very strong faith. She would push her shoes under her bed at night, which would assure she would kneel to find them each morning. This action reminded her to start each day with a prayer. Her name was Mary, and the first prayer she taught me in Lebanese was the Hail Mary."

Growing up in an entirely different culture, Leona, a thirty-eight-year-old engineering program manager, remembers a childhood steeped in Marian influences. In her native Ireland roadside grottos to the Blessed Mother dotted the countryside, and her primary school, named Mary Immaculate, began each class with a Hail Mary. Marian prayers even played a role in bringing Leona's parents together. She explains, "My parents always attended the novena of Our Lady of Lourdes in St. Mary's Church in Cork every February. This is where they first met, and apparently, over forty years ago, my mother said the novena that the cute guy with red hair would ask her out, and on the last night of the novena, my dad obliged! Dad tells the story and then ends with, 'Be careful what you pray for!'"

Even though Leona now lives far from her family, she still finds comfort in the Marian traditions they taught her. Back in Ireland, when she got her first car, her mother gave her a little statue of Mary and blessed the car with Lourdes water. Here in the United States, when Leona recently bought a new car, she put the same little statue in the glove compartment and blessed the vehicle with holy water. She gives her reason: "Even though my Mom was millions of miles away at the time, her presence was there as I asked Mary our Mother to protect me in my new car." Though Leona acknowledges that Mary does not play as large a part in her life as she used to, she continues to see her as a role model, a woman who, she says, "gives us perspective on how to live our lives with love." But she adds, "I still do pray to her for guidance, mostly when I am making major life decisions."

* * *

Praying for direction, as Leona and other women know, is comforting; it's a relief to know that we are not navigating life's paths on our own. All the same, discernment is rarely a straightforward process. When asking for guidance, few of us hear a voice in our ear or see a vision illuminating the future. Often the answers to our prayers are much more subtle, coming to us through the circumstances and people we encounter and unfolding gradually in our lives. This is as true of Marian prayers as of any other kind.

"Whenever I struggle, I always go to Mary," says Anna, a fashion designer. She explains, "I'm not a person who sees visions, but I always get my answer." The thirty-six-year-old has faced uncertainties that many of us would find unbearable. In 1987, just after finishing high school, she fled from the northern African nation of Eritrea, her homeland. Eritrea was torn by violence due to a long war with neighboring Ethiopia, and leaving could mean the difference between life and death. Anna's departure was difficult; by necessity, her plans to emigrate were kept secret, shared only with her family. All alone she flew to Greece, where she went to the American embassy and contacted her brother, who had previously escaped to the United States. She lived in Greece for a year, not knowing anyone there, waiting until her brother could make the necessary arrangements to bring her to America.

It was the beginning of a long period of adjustment. Anna eventually settled in San Francisco, where she struggled with a vastly different culture and with the separation from her loved ones. "I thought I'd never see my family again," she remembers. Between 1989 and 1993 their only contact was through letters because there was no phone connection between

Eritrea and other countries during the war. "I was always praying to Mary and to God, saying, maybe there would be a way to see my family and to talk to them," Anna recalls. Her prayers were finally answered; eventually, her parents and all of her siblings were able to leave Eritrea. All but two of them now live in the United States.

The experience of witnessing social violence firsthand has impacted Anna's spirituality. She is full of questions about the world and its many divisions: "Why are people suffering like this? Why are people different?" She finds herself asking God, "It's all your creation—all those different worlds—there's only one God who created all this. Why are there rich, why poor?" She has also wondered why her own life has been marked by struggle. At the same time, she knows that she is one of the fortunate ones. "I was very lucky. I have so many friends who didn't have the chance to leave," she says, adding that many of her classmates and friends died in their attempts to flee Eritrea.

Mary has always been a comforting figure in Anna's spiritual life, and a recent pilgrimage to Medjugorje has helped put some of her questions to rest. "Since I went to Medjugorje, my life has been peaceful, really peaceful. I used to worry a lot, but now I don't," she says. She describes the trip as being the most beautiful time of her life: "The first day I was just crying with no reason. The place was so peaceful I just didn't want to leave." Praying the rosary used to make her tired, but now it's become a daily practice. She explains, "I always have a rosary in my pocket, in my purse, because I believe Mary is with me to guide me."

Throughout the many upheavals of her life, Anna has found that Mary is always ready to give direction in one form or another. "I just have to say, 'OK, Mary, what's going on? You just have to tell me what to do.' She always gives me a way—God always sends someone to you," she says. The answer may not come quickly or in an obvious way, but it comes nonetheless, and the very act of prayer brings comfort. "I always wonder when people say, 'I saw Mary.' I don't see any visions or miracles, but always, when I pray to her, I feel so happy," Anna says. "When I pray especially deeply I feel really warm and peaceful." In a life that has been marked by uncertainty and struggle, such peace is truly the answer to a prayer.

* * *

When discussing Marian prayers, one of the first devotions that comes to mind is the rosary. With its circle of soothing Hail Marys, it appeals to many modern women, for whom life moves too quickly and quiet time is rare. "So many people today take classes on meditation, always looking for ways to relax and free the mind," says Rosemary, a fifty-eight-year-old executive assistant. "What we forget is the rosary! It is meditation!" Though her childhood experiences were less than enjoyable the rosary is now a rewarding part of her life. She remembers when it felt more like a punishment: "My cousin Kathleen Mary and I had to sit on chairs facing each other and say the rosary if we fought with each other." But now, she explains, "When I am in a stressful situation, fearful or angry, I say the Hail Mary—it takes the focus off of the moment, making me forget what else is going on in the world."

In addition to bringing peace, the rosary also has the effect of drawing women into a closer relationship with Mary. This was true for Sister Christine, a forty-one-year-old Dominican sister and young adult and campus minister. Years ago, before discerning her vocation, she was living and teaching in a small mining town in Arizona, where there were few young Catholics. "Recently returned to the church of my childhood, I was eager and enthusiastic about all things Catholic," she explains. "The little parish in this little town had an early morning daily Mass, and I found myself drawn to it. I'd go each day before getting ready for school and soon I noticed a little group of older women who were praying the rosary before the service. Soon I was going earlier than early to pray the rosary with them." Through these prayers, she developed a deep respect for Mary. Years later, after moving to the Phoenix area, her rosary, she says, "fell a bit silent for a while," though she still prayed it during Advent and Lent. "Each time I did, I became reacquainted with Mary and her role in my life. She was silent but strong for me," she remembers. "A peace would surround me when I was in more regular contact with her."

As Christine's own faith journey progressed, she found herself questioning the traditional portrayal of Mary as a "meek, quiet, obedient woman." Slowly, this image began to change. She explains, "Over time, I came to see Mary as a strong and powerful advocate and disciple. Today, I think of Mary as a friend, companion, and model." With this new image of Mary, the experience of praying the rosary has deepened, becoming not just about peace but about connection with a woman who shares Christine's spiritual journey. "Today when I pray the rosary I know I'm praying *with* Mary, not *to* Mary," she says. "I know I'm asking her to stand with me in the presence of God and to hold my hand in times of sorrow and petition. She's stronger than I ever thought possible and her strength is contagious."

* * *

Though the mysteries of the rosary include some of the most significant moments in Mary's life—the Annunciation, the Visitation and the Assumption, among others—their primary purpose is to draw us into relationship with Christ. As Pope John Paul II wrote in his letter *Rosarium Virginis Mariae*, "To recite the rosary is nothing other than to *contemplate with Mary the face of Christ*."[2] As many women have learned, by meditating upon the events of Christ's life, he becomes more fully present in our own.

For Maria, a healthcare administrator, the rosary did more than simply deepen her connection to Christ: It created it. In fact, the rosary was the bridge that helped Maria overcome the seemingly insurmountable distance between Jesus and herself. "I got to know Mary because I was afraid of Jesus," says the thirty-six-year-old convert. Though she was in an RCIA program, deepening her spiritual life as she prepared to become Catholic, she felt haunted by regrets over choices in her past. "I didn't know how to reconcile my sins," she explains. "No matter how hard I tried to suppress them they would surface in my thoughts and dreams." Because of her past, she was afraid to pray to Jesus directly. "I was terrified that he would reject me," she says.

One night, Maria heard a talk on Mary, which inspired her to learn the rosary. She began to pray it every morning. "Each time that I prayed the rosary, I was learning about Jesus through the mysteries, but I still felt distant from him," she recalls. "I prayed for Mary to show me the way."

One Sunday morning—the day of the Mass for the Elect, in which the RCIA candidates are formally presented to the archbishop—Maria woke up feeling that Mary was telling her to mourn her past. "After praying the rosary, I felt led to pray to Jesus and ask, 'What does Mary want me to mourn?' Then, I saw Jesus. In my mind, I saw him on a beach." She sat with him on the beach for a while, then asked him what she should mourn. "As soon as I asked, tremendous grief and sorrow came over me," she remembers. "I began to sob uncontrollably. I realized that I was grieving over my sins." She felt Jesus ask her to let go of her pain and grief, and she recalls, "this fiery ball came out of me and Jesus held it in his hands. Immediately, I felt all the pain and sadness and grief leave my body. He threw the ball of fire into the ocean, and said, 'Look, it's being swallowed by the water. It's gone. I've gotten rid of it for you.'" Maria describes feeling an "immense love, greater than I've ever felt in my life."

Maria is grateful to Mary for bringing her close to Christ. She says, "With Mary's help, I got to know Jesus in a tremendously loving way and he took away my pain. I couldn't believe that Mary had given me such a beautiful gift." With Jesus now so real to her, Maria says that the intensity of Mary's presence has lessened. All the same, the Blessed Mother is never far away. "I know through the rosary that Mary is always with us during our time of need," she says. "Like a loving mother, she keeps an eye on all her children, and when necessary, she makes her presence known. When I call on Jesus, occasionally it's Mary that answers me."

* * *

While women like Maria have found that the rosary brings them closer to Christ, it can also have the effect of bringing women closer to each other. Though it is often prayed individually, group recitations of the rosary offer a chance for Catholics to connect with their larger faith community. No one knows this better than Marcia, forty-seven, whose own personal journey with the rosary has blossomed into a network of prayer and unity, bringing together people of different ages and backgrounds.

Marcia first began to pray the rosary in 2000, when she worked as a consultant for the New York Board of Trade at the World Trade Center. Each day, as she took the express bus back home to New Jersey, she would pull out a booklet that guided her through the mysteries and prayers. "Gradually, I became familiar with each mystery and which mystery was associated with each day of the week," she says. "I loved reflecting on how strong Mary's faith in God was and how her 'yes' changed the world—forever." Ironically, Marcia's work on Wall Street has twice put her in situations requiring strong faith of her own. In 1993, she was working in the World Trade Center during the first terrorist attack. Eight years later, on September 11, 2001, Marcia relived the nightmare as she fled from her office in the doomed towers. She remembers the day well and how she got through it: "As I walked away from the buildings, I prayed the rosary. I remember crying out to the Holy Spirit to lead me to safety and then to Mary for strength and trust. She is with me as I continue my (sometimes) daily struggle to heal."

The months following 9/11 were difficult ones. The financial sector took an economic hit and Marcia lost her job; emotionally, she was still feeling the aftershocks of her experience. That Christmas, she found a special comfort in praying the rosary at night, after the family had gone to bed. "It seemed the more I took time to contemplate Mary's trials and struggles, the more I could lift up my own challenges as well as my joys to my Mother. This very special time with Mary helped prepare my heart and my soul for the joy and celebration of the birth of Jesus. It was beautiful and peaceful and intimate and sacred," she says.

Marcia was inspired to teach her two daughters to pray the rosary. Soon, the entire family was praying it together: in the living room, in the car, as they walked their dog. Marcia then had the idea to invite her friends and their daughters for a monthly "mother/daughter" rosary. "Many of them eagerly agreed," says Marcia. She goes on, "Some confided in me that they hadn't prayed the rosary since they were children. Others never learned how to pray the rosary. So I told them we would learn together!" The group began meeting in March of 2002, and soon it took on an energy of its own: "Friends began bringing neighbors and relatives. Sometimes we had three generations of women praying together. We moved furniture, had people on chairs, floors and even sitting on the steps leading to the second floor." In time, the group expanded to include men as well, becoming what she calls "a family rosary." With the help of a speakerphone, the circle has grown even larger; friends and family from out of town have been able to participate in the prayers. Now, approximately 150 people receive Marcia's e-mails about the rosary meetings. "On average we have between thirty to fifty people every month that come to our home to honor Our Lady and seek her intercession, her aid and to thank her for her protection and blessings," she says.

Mary continues to bless Marcia with protection and healing. In 2005, on the fourth anniversary of 9/11, Marcia spent some time praying in front of the Blessed Sacrament. "Wherever Jesus is, Mary is too, and it was through Mary's love that I surrendered the memories of that day. It was an amazing healing for me," she says. Wherever life takes us, Marcia is convinced that Mary is there, always guiding us to her Son and showing us how to live in the service of others. "Mary teaches me about practicing charity and patience and how to give myself away for love of others. She also teaches me about faithfulness and fortitude—in bountiful times of joy and celebration and in times of sorrow, pain and grief," she says. Thanks to Marcia's rosary meetings, others are also discovering Mary as a model disciple, learning that a circle of beads can be a powerful way to build a life of faith.

* * *

One of the beauties of a personal prayer life is that there is always room to grow. Prayers that we learned as children sometimes fade into the background as we grow up and find new ways to connect with the divine. Conversely, as adults we sometimes circle back to the prayers we learned in our younger years, reclaiming them and making them our own. Often, too, the direction of our prayers changes over time. Mary can be a cherished advocate at some points in our lives; at other times, the need for her intercession may lessen.

Emily, a twenty-four-year-old administrative assistant, is very aware of the evolution of her prayer life, particularly with regard to Mary. Growing up, she was taught to see the Blessed Mother as a powerful advocate. Her mother would tell her, "Mary is an intercessor for our prayers, and so just imagine that your prayer is like a bushel of apples. When you bring them to Mary, she bakes them into an apple pie and she brings the apple pie to Jesus. It's like she takes the prayers and makes them sweeter, so it's harder for him to say no." Emily recalls that she liked that image: "I always thought that was cute, so if I really wanted something I'd pray to Mary, because I always thought, Jesus will listen to her better than he'll listen to me."

In spite of this, though, Emily did not enjoy the obligatory family rosary nights. "I remember I'd be outside, it would be a nice warm summer night, and we had a ton of kids in the neighborhood, and I'd be outside playing. My mom would open the door and she would yell at the top of her lungs, 'It's time for the rosary.' We would have to come inside, stop what we were doing." The house had a huge window facing the street, and Emily's mother would turn off the lights and light candles to create a prayerful atmosphere. "I resented the candles because it just drew attention and all the kids could see through the window. I remember as I got older, it would get harder and harder." Because of this, the rosary came to feel like a duty for Emily.

As an adult, Emily has been on a conscious journey to deepen her relationship with God. Now, she cares more about discerning God's will for her than about what she calls "treating God like Santa Claus." She's come to realize that, in prayer, "the most important thing is just being in God's presence and trying to surrender your own will so you can allow his to work in you. I don't think I've really come around to that when I pray to Mary." She explains that praying the rosary is still a challenge for her, a practice that feels like "going through the motions." She adds, "I know intellectually that when I'm praying the rosary my intentions are being heard and that Mary is taking care of me, or whomever I'm praying for. I know that intellectually, but I don't think I've really realized it spiritually."

Interestingly, though, she envisions a time when she can see herself developing a deeper relationship with Mary. "I think that when I'm a mother and a wife it'll force me to think less of myself and more of my family. In those moments I think I'm going to be reaching out for a model of how to be a good mother and a good wife. I can really see relating to Mary in those times." As she has learned, one "can't just sit back and will a relationship to happen. That relationship with Mary, like anybody, has to come through an open heart and actually putting in the work of prayer and being open-minded about the whole thing." She acknowledges that though she used to blame her mother's obligatory rosaries for her lack of connection to Mary, she doesn't anymore. "That's ridiculous. No parent can give you a perfect version of anything," she says. Rather, she now gives her mom credit, saying, "the only reason I have a desire for that at all is because she did expose me to it." For now, her relationship with Mary remains a work in progress. "I know who Mary is, and I have a desire to know her more, but I realize it's just probably going to take me some time."

Emily's story would no doubt resonate with Lu, a ninety-two-year-old mother of six. Her own life is an example of how a connection with Mary, and a personal love of the rosary, can unfold gradually over time. "As a child, there was no special feeling toward Mary; she was just a woman who gave birth to Jesus," she recalls. "My Catholic faith formation, of which the rosary became a part, was rather sporadic." For most of

Lu's life, the rosary has been what she calls "here and there rather than a source of strength regularly." In high school she prayed it with her parish young women's group; later, she and her husband would pick up their beads "occasionally but not regularly." At one point, when her children were young, she attempted to have them say the rosary before school. "It seemed a good thing to do, but hardly the best time of day and we soon gave it up."

It's only recently that the rosary has become a daily, cherished part of Lu's life. "For over the past year, or maybe two, I have been saying just one decade before going to bed. It takes me ten to fifteen minutes to say just one, because each word has so much meaning that I say the words slowly. Since I follow the four sets of mysteries, the life of Jesus is played out in my mind and heart over and over," she says. She loves the Luminous Mysteries, added by Pope John Paul II in 2002. "I find these Luminous Mysteries provide a more complete history of Jesus' time on Earth rather than jumping from the young Jesus found in the temple straight to the beginning of his suffering and death," she says. Among the events of Jesus' life, she is inspired by the story of the miracle at Cana, particularly for what it reveals about Mary and her initiative. "I love the fact that her relationship with Jesus had become rather easygoing by the time of the marriage feast at Cana," she explains. "She could ignore his protest at the timing, and simply tell the servants to follow his orders! She was pretty cool!"

As Lu reflects on her journey with the rosary, she shares a story that adds a new layer of meaning to her nightly decades. Lu's mother died at age seventy-five, and after her death Lu found a surprising letter with a request. "Among her papers, she had written her bequest to her children: a decade of the rosary daily for each one, and a request that we continue it for ourselves. Come to think of it," Lu says, "I'm finally doing that." As her story shows, it's never too late to embrace a new—or, in fact, an old—way to pray.

* * *

In talking to these women, I've been struck by the diversity of their experiences of Marian prayer. The prayers can be meditative, lulling women into peace; they can also be active, pulling women into the lives of Mary and her Son. There's a deeply private quality to the rosary, making it a very personal devotion; there's also a power in praying it as a group, feeling the combined energy of a community. In the end, it's obvious that there is no "right" way to pray. Each of us has her own personal spiritual life, one that may or may not include Mary as a regular advocate. Still, there's no question that the Blessed Mother has something unique to offer us. She's the mother who cares for our spiritual growth, the woman who understands the rhythms of a female life. Above all, she's the faithful disciple who is always ready to drop everything, take us by the hand, and leads us where she wants us to be: close to her son.

| MARY OF THE APPARITIONS: A MOTHER WHO REACHES OUT |

...I am your merciful mother and the mother of all the nations that live on this earth who would love me, who would speak with me, who would search for me, and who would place their confidence in me. There I will hear their laments and remedy and cure all their miseries, misfortunes, and sorrows. (Our Lady of Guadalupe to Juan Diego) [1]

As a child, I loved visiting my grandparents' church. While my own church was a boxy modern structure, theirs was a graceful 1920s building in a vaguely Spanish style. Its stained-glass windows glowed with jewel colors and clearly recognizable figures: Saint Agnes, Saint Patrick in his green robes, Mary and the apostles at Pentecost. There were lovely statues, too: Saint Thérèse with her armful of roses, the Infant of Prague in his stiff dress. Most fascinating of all, at the front of the church and hidden off to the side was a circular alcove lined with gray-blue satin. A light illuminated the large statue within: Our Lady of Fatima, dressed in white robes edged with gold. Her feet were bare and rosaries were draped over her hands. She was bent at the waist, inclined forward, as if leaning to hear the prayers offered from the kneeler before her. Her head was tilted slightly to the side, which also gave her the appearance of listening intently. Her eyes were dark brown, warm and deep.

After Mass one Sunday, when I was very young, my grandmother walked my sister and me up to the front of the church to look at the shrine. In my mind's eye I can see Grandma, a little girl on each hand, approaching the alcove with hushed reverence. I sense that she loved to see

Mary through our eyes, eyes that were wide with wonder at the celestial beauty in front of us. Mary seemed so real as she stood on her pedestal, vases of flowers at her feet. She leaned in as if she wanted to connect with us, two little girls in our Sunday clothes, just as she had reached out to three peasant children decades before. She was there, close enough to touch, near enough to captivate our senses and imagination.

"Isn't she beautiful?" whispered my grandmother.

* * *

Many of our most cherished images of Mary come from the apparitions. There's Our Lady of Guadalupe, in her blue cloak dotted with stars; there's Our Lady of Lourdes, with yellow roses on her feet, hovering in her niche in the grotto. The image of Mary as she appeared to Saint Catherine Labouré in 1830 is imprinted on the Miraculous Medal, surely one of the most ubiquitous depictions of the Blessed Mother. These moments when Mary came back to Earth have become deeply ingrained in the Catholic imagination, inspiring pilgrimages and prompting millions of prayers.

At the same time, many Catholics are not quite sure what to think of Marian apparitions. These miraculous visits often seem starkly at odds with the realities of daily life and with human knowledge of science and logic. For its part, the church hierarchy proceeds cautiously when investigating reports of an alleged visitation. For an apparition to be pronounced worthy of belief, it must undergo intense scrutiny and evaluation. The number of visitations that have been formally approved by the church are but a fraction of the apparitions reported throughout history.

Church teaching helps clear up the confusion about how to integrate apparitions into our Catholic beliefs. Even those that have received the approval of the church—including Fatima, Lourdes and Guadalupe—are not considered to be binding elements of our faith. Mary's messages to individuals are considered "private revelation," not "public revelation" like the teachings of Christ and the apostles. Individuals are free to believe in these Marian apparitions if they wish, says the church, but such belief is not a necessary component of a Catholic faith.

All the same, it's clear that these visitations have a deep emotional resonance with many Catholics. On a narrative level, apparition stories have both drama and a delicious mysteriousness, one that alternately enthralled and scared me as a child. On a deeper level, I suspect that these stories touch the hearts of many Catholics because of what they say about Mary. This is not a woman who stays comfortably ensconced in heaven, watching from a distance, but one who ventures forth to meet us on our own turf. Her messages to pray for peace are reminders for us to return faith to the center of our busy, distracted lives. The apparitions are also consistent with her role as mother: Mary knows we need her help even when we aren't aware of it ourselves. Like any good mother, she also knows just what to do to get our attention.

Some Catholic women describe having a strong childhood connection to the apparitions. Alberta, a sixty-two-year-old former elementary school teacher, remembers a family outing to the movies that planted the seed of her love for Mary. The movie was about Fatima, Portugal, one of the most well-known apparition sites. It was in Fatima that Mary appeared to three peasant children in 1917, urging them to pray the rosary for peace and conversion. The film made a deep impression on Alberta, largely because the visionaries were children. "What I got out of this movie was that if Mary was talking to kids, and I was a kid, just look at what they were being asked to do. This message was meant for me too!" she says. "So I think this is where any real devotion to Mary started for me."

Alberta's experience touches on a common thread running through the apparition stories: the humble status of those whom Mary visits. Often, she appears to children or young teenagers, as in Fatima or Lourdes. At other times, she comes to the disenfranchised or the marginalized, as with the indigenous Juan Diego in Mexico. Few of her apparitions are directed at people with wealth and privilege. In fact, those who have power are often the ones who mock, bully or threaten the visionaries once the apparitions are made public. In this way, Mary's visits reaffirm the words she said upon visiting Elizabeth: The lowly are lifted up while the strong are sent away empty.

Although Melissa, thirty, doesn't identify Mary as being a big part of her spiritual life, she does feel that the apparitions have helped her understand Mary's relationship with the world. "I do not think about Mary or pray to her as much as others would," says the chartered accountant. "My visit to Fatima in July 2005 did give me a renewed sense of appreciation for Mary's powers and abilities, though. And, of course, she is a mother above all. This was especially apparent to me when I was in Fatima and could feel how she really blessed and looked after the three children she appeared to, even though two of them died when they were still really young." Melissa also believes that Mary's decision to appear to young people is absolutely consistent with Christ's teaching about how to attain heavenly peace. "I believe Mary shows true compassion to the children that we must all be like in order to enter the kingdom of heaven," she says. "That touches something inside of me—a need to be more humble and childlike."

Like Melissa, Lucy, a thirty-eight-year-old cosmetologist, was touched by a visit to Fatima. In Lucy's case, however, the pilgrimage built upon an already solid devotion to Our Lady. Lucy was born in Portugal, where Mary's appearance is celebrated every year with a big "festa." "You participate for the entire week; that's how I was first introduced to Fatima," she explains. "We line the streets with fresh flowers, carpets of flowers, and we have rosaries at people's houses." Traditionally, bread, wine and meat are given to the poor, and a huge state of Our Lady of Fatima is carried in the processions. "People make promises—promises to walk the entire length of the procession on their knees or barefoot, carrying the statues," Lucy says. When she was a child, her family moved to California and settled in an area with a large Portuguese community. Their participation in the festas continued in their new home, and Lucy's father still plays in the band that marches in the parades.

Lucy's connection to Our Lady of Fatima is rooted not just in community celebrations, but also in her family's most deeply felt sorrows and joys. Her parents' first child, a daughter, was stillborn. They named her

Fatima. Three more children followed, two girls and a boy, named for the three children to whom Mary appeared: Lucy, Francisco and Jacinta. Sadly, Jacinta died when she was only a few hours old. Lucy points out that this is an echo of the fate of the first Jacinta, who died of influenza when she was still a child.

With such personal roots in the Fatima story, Lucy's visit to the shrine several years ago was the fulfillment of a long-held wish. She describes the overwhelming sense of faith and mystery that she felt upon visiting the apparition site. "I don't care what you believe in, but every hair on your body will stand up," she says. She describes seeing "women and men walking on their knees." She recalls, "their bleeding and their suffering" and expresses her awe at how they "believe in [Mary] so much." She truly felt the sacredness of the site, one that seems to inspire the finest in human behavior. "They have a box there that you put money into for candles. It's stuffed with money, but no one would ever think of stealing it—and we're not talking about a rich country here."

As an adult, Lucy reflects that turning to Mary has become instinctive. "I do pray to Mary, almost every day," she says. "When something goes wrong, I say, 'Our Lady' in Portuguese." She hopes that her children will grow up with the same close connection to Our Lady of Fatima, the "wonderful woman" who has walked with her family both in celebration and struggle.

* * *

In 1531, in Tepeyac, Mexico, Mary appeared to Juan Diego. She spoke of her love and compassion for him and all people, and asked that a church be built on the very site where she was standing. Juan Diego attempted to pass her message along to the bishop, who responded with dismissive skepticism. Eventually the bishop demanded proof of the visitation, which Mary provided by making roses bloom in the December frost. Juan Diego gathered the roses in his *tilma*, or cloak, with Mary's instructions to show them only to the bishop. When he opened his cloak for the bishop and the roses tumbled out, both men were astonished at what was revealed.

The cloak bore the very image of Mary as she had appeared to Juan Diego: a young, dark-skinned woman in a salmon robe, wearing the black sash of pregnancy, with her hands clasped in prayer. Known as Our Lady of Guadalupe, it has since become one of the most beloved images of the Blessed Mother.

"Since I was very small, I have felt a connection to the Virgin of Guadalupe. Somehow, she just looked more real to me," says Mary, a forty-two-year-old elementary school teacher. As a child, Mary never felt drawn to the pale blue-and-white statues of the Blessed Mother, the "translucent-looking lady." Our Lady of Guadalupe, however, struck a chord with her: "She made more sense to me. I found her really beautiful." Growing up in California's Central Valley, home to a large Mexican population, Mary saw this image everywhere, and her reaction to it was almost visceral. "Every time I'd see something with the Virgin of Guadalupe on it, it would captivate me. If it was a postcard, I'd buy it; I had T-shirts with the Virgin of Guadalupe on them." Though Mary herself did not pray to Our Lady of Guadalupe, she always sensed that she was intensely sympathetic to suffering. "I knew if she were an icon to the people of Mexico and the Mexican families I know, and if people kept going back to her, there had to be something there," she says.

At age thirty-four, Mary was blindsided by terrible news: She was diagnosed with uterine cancer and given a 20 percent chance of survival. Suddenly, everything in her life was different. "One month, you think everything is fine, and the next month, you have your uterus removed, you've been given giant doses of chemotherapy, and you're just trying to grapple with the fact that you can never have your own children, also dealing with the fact that you may lose your life," she says. "And it's a cancer that no one my age usually gets, so it's very hard to find peace or a place to rest anywhere in your mind or body when that's happening." In the midst of her fear, she needed the comfort of prayer, but found a barrier in praying to God. She was grappling with the question of why she had the cancer—had God caused it? Was it his will that she suffer and perhaps die?

Was it some kind of punishment he was giving her? "I didn't know who God was at that moment," she says.

In the midst of these questions, she found herself turning to the Blessed Mother for comfort. "I knew this was the best person who could possibly intercede," she says. When she approached Mary, there were no spiritual barriers. "I just felt a wave of listening and compassion come over me and almost felt understanding from her, and I suddenly felt as if I could pray. It was really important to have that female to talk to." Mary was comforted to think that the Blessed Mother knew the pain she was going through at being unable to have children of her own. "All of a sudden, I felt like someone understood—not that Jesus couldn't, but in my limited human way at the time, I needed to talk to a woman."

Although the initial prognosis for recovery had been far from positive, Mary's cancer went into remission. Gradually, she regained her health. Four years after the diagnosis, she took a trip to Mexico City, an experience that she describes as "extra-special." There, she visited the basilica of Our Lady of Guadalupe, where Juan Diego's *tilma* is on display, its colors unfaded over four centuries later. It was a visit that made Mary reflect on faith, on prayer and on her own journey. "You look at the cloak, and you're like, 'How could that happen?' At the same time, just knowing that she's the patron saint of Mexico and just knowing that that site was such a holy site, I felt like it was an auspicious occasion and that the prayers I said there would be blessed. It was just an amazing experience." One year later, she passed the five-year cancer-free mark, which her friends and family celebrated by throwing her a large party.

Now, eight years after the cancer, Our Lady of Guadalupe is still a cherished part of Mary's life. She also has a habit of turning up in unexpected places; Mary recently attended a bar mitzvah party, and the Jewish woman who hosted it had images of the Virgin of Guadalupe all over the house. When Mary commented on them, the woman said, "I just love her—I don't know why, but I just feel attached to her. I love her." Mary's own journey makes this an easy phenomenon to understand. "I think women need a powerful image of a heavenly mother they can connect to—someone you can really talk to because she would know your heart," she muses. Our Lady of Guadalupe has always had a unique place in Mary's heart, and it's equally clear that Mary has a special place in hers. "I feel like she's always been watching out for me," Mary says.

* * *

For many Catholics, Marian apparition sites are tightly linked to the idea of healing. The places where Mary came to Earth are usually viewed as holy ground, charged with the promise of heavenly power and divine intervention. Nowhere is this more true than at Lourdes, France, where in 1858 Mary appeared repeatedly to Bernadette Soubirous, a young peasant girl. At Mary's instruction, Bernadette dug in the dirt, uncovering a spring. Thousands of medical miracles have since been attributed to the spring's healing waters; of these cures, sixty-seven have been officially recognized as miracles by the church. With 5 million visitors a year, Lourdes is one of the largest pilgrimage sites in the world.

It's also a site that prompts reflection about what, exactly, it means to be healed. Not everyone who bathes in the springs at Lourdes ends up being physically cured. Though modern pilgrims recognize this fact, they come nonetheless, as if challenging the notion that there is only one kind of healing. Is there something in the mere act of making the journey that offers spiritual comfort? Does the acceptance of one's illness or infirmity constitute its own kind of miracle? Apart from physical cures, what are the other, more subtle kinds of healing that Lourdes provides?

For Andrea, an eating disorder activist, Lourdes has been a life-giving place on many levels. The thirty-five-year-old was raised Catholic, and grew up with admiration for the lovely image of Mary that was celebrated during May processions. "I remember she was so beautiful that it made you feel all warm inside," she says. In high school she drifted away from the church, only to reconnect with it when she was nineteen. With the help of a mentor and supportive church community, she "fell in love" with her faith and with Jesus, though she struggled to truly understand Mary.

At this time, Andrea was also in the grips of another, more severe struggle: She was battling anorexia, an eating disorder that would prove very difficult to overcome.

In the summer of 2000, Andrea's good friend Dianna was dying of cancer, and made a pilgrimage to Lourdes. Andrea explains that Dianna was clearly hoping for a miracle. "I, on the other hand, prayed the novenas for her along with the parish, my rosary in hand, with great skepticism," she recalls. "I always felt people created what they wanted to see and hear within the great apparitions of Mary." Returning home from Lourdes, Dianna was still very ill, but Andrea was inspired to see how graciously she accepted her inevitable death. Dianna also brought a special message for Andrea. "She told me that as she was at Lourdes in the baths, she had a vision of me working there. She then made me promise that I go minister in her name after she passed," recalls Andrea. "I wanted only to bring her peace at this time, and agreed."

For nearly a year after Dianna's death, Andrea dragged her feet about keeping the promise. Finally, the nudging of a priest friend inspired her to make it happen. Friends donated frequent-flier miles, and Andrea raised funds and arranged lodging at a convent. The logistics of the trip were complicated, but Andrea was motivated by the memory of the support that Dianna had shown her during her struggles with anorexia, the disorder that was still a part of Andrea's life.

When Andrea arrived in Lourdes, she immediately understood why Dianna had been so adamant that she make the trip. "It was a magnificently special place," Andrea says. "My first day as I walked along the river path covered in leaves toward the grotto, I could feel a peace I never knew." Her work assisting the pilgrims at the grotto spring would also be a new experience, not just for Andrea but for the Lourdes community: It was the first time a woman had been placed in that particular job. "I knew right away this meant something, and I knew Dianna was by my side."

Andrea vividly remembers the sights and sounds of her first day at the grotto. "For two and a half hours I watched people come and pray before

Mary. I helped them walk through this 'cave' of sorts, paying their respects, their sincere gratitude. They stared up at the statue with glistening eyes, they passed their worn rosary beads along the water-dripped rock, and they carried their candles and mumbled in their own foreign tongues, 'Thank you, dear Lady, thank you.'" Witnessing this devotion, Andrea felt the distance between herself and Mary slip away. "I began to pray to Mary from that day forward," she says. "I asked her questions, sitting in silence for the answers. I asked others about their devotion. I reread all the stories of her in the Bible. I found a friend."

It was upon returning from Lourdes that Andrea began her own journey of healing. It wasn't easy; years of anorexia had taken a physical and emotional toll. But the power of Lourdes, and the memory of the friend who brought her there, helped sustain her. "I had a severe crash at one point, and upon returning to Lourdes had some serious prayer time and reflection with Our Lady," Andrea explains. The fruit of this experience was her decision to embrace the philosophy that Dianna had always believed: "Fight. Fight for life. Choose life. Live life…because you are loved." Andrea now returns to Lourdes yearly, a pilgrimage that helps her reconnect with Mary's strength and inspires her to pattern her own life after that fierce resolve. "This woman, this amazing, strong woman had a voice," she says. "I promised myself to always use my voice."

Though Dianna's pilgrimage to Lourdes did not result in her own physical recovery, it opened a pathway for Andrea's healing journey. Now, in her work as an activist speaking out on eating disorders, Andrea is using her voice to reach others. She knows that Mary is supporting her in her own struggles, just as she supports millions of other people on their unique journeys. "Mary is many things to many people. That is what is so special about her," she reflects. "She is what she is meant to be for each person. This is why she has so many titles. This is why we never stop asking the great questions about her." Andrea explains that she does not feel called to visit any other apparition sites; Lourdes was all it took for her to connect with Mary. "I know who she is for me, and this is what we each need to discover," she says. "Our faith journey is no one else's, but our very own."

* * *

For all their mysterious qualities, I suspect that the apparitions appeal to us mainly because they are so concrete. At an apparition site, we can touch the place where Mary stood, passing our hands over the rock of a grotto. We can marvel at the colors and textures of a cloak forever bearing her image. We can bathe in the waters of a spring, our minds open to whatever kind of healing we may receive. In doing so, we have tangible reassurance that Mary is our advocate, the loving mother who is always engaged with her children's lives. For my part, I find it comforting to think of Mary coming to Earth, leaving paradise to intervene in our messy lives. Though faith can sometimes feel like a one-sided stretch toward something remote, the apparitions are dramatic reminders that heaven does in fact reach back, meeting us right where we are.

| IMMACULATE MARY: PERFECTION AND VIRGINITY |

"I am the Immaculate Conception."
–Our Lady of Lourdes to Saint Bernadette

...Holy Virgin of virgins,
Mother of Christ,
Mother of the Church,
Mother of divine grace,
Mother most pure,
Mother most chaste,
Mother inviolate,
Mother undefiled ...
(From the Litany of Loreto)

Thanks to the teachers at St. Simon Elementary School, I grew up knowing a tremendous amount about my Catholic faith. I knew the names of saints and sacraments; I memorized the Apostles' Creed and absorbed the lessons of the parables. I also learned something that many Catholics never do: the true meaning of the Immaculate Conception. Lots of people think that this refers to Jesus, and how he was conceived without sin, but they're wrong, our teachers told us. It really refers to Mary. Because Jesus grew inside Mary's womb, they explained, she too had to be sinless. As a result, God made sure that she was conceived without any mark of original sin. From the beginning of her life until the end, she was absolutely perfect.

As a child, this was never a difficult concept for me. I accepted Mary's sinlessness readily, and had no reason to question it. In fact, the feast day of the Immaculate Conception, December 8, always had pleasant associations for me. It was a school holiday, and every year my mother and grandparents would take my sister and me to downtown San Francisco for Christmas window-shopping. Because of this, the eighth of December was not a time for me to reflect on Mary's perfection. Instead, it was a festive day when I ate breakfast at Sears Fine Foods, marveled at the Renaissance dress of the doorman at the Sir Francis Drake Hotel, and pressed my nose against the holiday windows at Gump's.

Only later did I consciously ponder Mary's sinlessness. In college and my early twenties, when I was looking at Catholicism with a critical eye, Mary's immaculate nature became problematic. I still believed that she had been conceived without sin, but that perfection created a barrier between her and me. Somehow, sinlessness equaled difference; sinlessness equaled judgment; sinlessness equaled a gap that I couldn't bridge. At that time, my image of Mary had not moved beyond the lovely blue-and-white lady with outstretched arms who stood on a pedestal high in the corner of my elementary school classrooms. That statue was an apt metaphor for her: She was above all of us, unreachable and unreal in her perfection.

* * *

In my work on this book, I found that many women were very conscious of Mary's sinlessness. Nancy, a sixty-five-year-old homemaker, explains that she thinks of Mary as "a person who hasn't done anything wrong," and that the quality she most associates with Mary is the word "immaculate." Though she does pray to Mary for guidance, she also feels a tangible distance between the Blessed Mother and herself. "As I've gotten older, I wonder why Mary had to be set apart from all the rest of us," Nancy reflects. "Why did she have to be the Blessed Virgin Mary? Why couldn't Jesus' mother be like any other woman?"

Nancy's questions point to the challenge that many women face: There's Mary, and then there are the rest of us. By reason of her sinlessness, the Blessed Mother is immediately removed from everything we understand about humanity. After all, none of us has ever met a perfect person. What would such a woman be like? How are we to understand a person who is exempt from the fumbling mistakes and the misguided choices that are so much a part of the human condition? How can such a woman possibly be real to us?

Donna, a fifty-six-year-old elementary school music teacher, finds it a challenge to envision the kind of woman Mary was. "I've always had just a little bit of a struggle with seeing Mary as a real live woman, wife and mother versus her being sinless and perfect," she says. "Didn't she sometimes get impatient with Joseph when he didn't come in to dinner when she called him? I guess she could get annoyed without getting angry, wherein lies the difference between Mary and me." Donna recalls that one of her father's favorite hymns was the song "Hail Mary, Gentle Woman." "It makes me smile every time I hear or sing it, because *it's so not me*," she says. "No one would *ever* call me 'quiet light' or 'peaceful dove.' Raging eagle, maybe, peaceful dove, no."[1] In spite of the differences between Mary and herself, Donna still regards the Blessed Mother as a friend and ally. "I feel like she's on my side," she says. "I'm counting on her to help me when I cross over!"

For some women, Mary's perfection raises questions about how to approach her in prayer. What is the proper way to speak to a woman who is sinless? Do we need to mask our flawed selves and rough edges in order to communicate with her? Karen, a thirty-nine-year-old teacher who never hesitates to share her thoughts with her friends, describes the challenges she used to find in praying to such an immaculate figure. "I remember praying to her as a child and feeling judged," she says. "I can't believe I can remember this, but one time I remember praying to her in a candid fashion. I couldn't stop thinking, 'She must think I'm crazy or maybe even disrespectful.' I felt guilty to approach her so casually and openly, and I wondered if she could be forgiving of my nonchalant approach because she could see and understand my true character. She just seemed so perfect that I felt intimidated by that."

For other women, Mary's sinlessness gives rise to feelings of frustration and resentment. Throughout history, Catholic women have often been told, both directly and indirectly, to pattern themselves after Mary.

Her status as *the* role model for female Catholics raises a host of questions. If she had the special privilege of being born without sin, many women think, then how can we possibly hope to emulate her? Why are we even told to try? To some, the message that they should be like Mary seems like a setup for failure, or a way for women to be made to feel guilty about their own imperfection. The fact that such messages have traditionally come from male clergy makes the issue all the more emotionally charged. As a result, many women have come to regard Mary as a kind of pawn, a figure used by men to keep women from getting too comfortable with themselves.

I can understand this because I myself, in the past, have felt a kind of resentment toward Mary. It's similar to the resentment one might feel toward an older sibling who can do no wrong: The more you are told you should pattern yourself after someone perfect, the harder it is to develop an authentic relationship with that person. He or she becomes not a real human being but an impossible standard, a passive Goody Two-shoes. To many Catholics, Mary is more a plaster statue than a flesh-and-blood woman. How does one rescue her from this image? How can we understand and embrace her full humanity?

Lucia, a sixty-eight-year-old iconographer, offers one perspective. Though she herself has never viewed Mary as a passive figure, conversations with women who do have helped her forge her own understanding of the Blessed Mother. It's an understanding that has developed over the course of many years. Growing up in the Episcopal church, Lucia had no formal knowledge of Mary; she describes her family as being "very 'Protestant' in its approach to worship and tradition." She explains, "Anything Catholic was viewed with deep suspicion. Mary definitely fell into that category." A small statue from the Christmas crèche, and the infancy narratives from the King James Bible, were all she knew of Jesus' mother. In spite of this limited exposure—or perhaps because of it— Lucia's interest in Mary was piqued. "I was definitely curious about her because she was mysterious," Lucia explains. She even memorized the

"Hail Mary" from a book, and recited it to herself when she was alone.

Later, when Lucia discovered, what she deemed the "high church," Anglo-Catholic side of the Episcopal faith, she began to learn more about Mary. In the years that followed, she became aware of the ambivalence that many Catholic women felt toward her. On the one hand, she noticed that many of them felt a connection to the Blessed Mother; on the other, Lucia witnessed their anger at the way Mary had seemingly been appropriated by men for purposes of their own. Though Lucia could understand their frustration with some of the messages directed at women over the centuries, she believed that Mary was far more than a two-dimensional figure. "Once I was grown and married and had some life experience behind me, the traditional colorless notion of a 'passive' Mary made less and less sense," she says. When she was in her late thirties, she recalls being on a Cursillo team with a nun who "raged at the pope for citing the Blessed Mother as a role model for women." It was a stand that was hard for Lucia to understand. "I could find no common ground with her because her idea of Our Lady was that colorless, passive figure I'd never met," she explains. "When leaders in the women's movement tried to come up with an alternative image, the result was reminiscent of a type of aggressive political activist with which I was all too familiar. I knew that was just as wrong, only at the opposite extreme."

In the late nineties, Lucia's spiritual path led her to a crossroads. "Our children were grown and as often happens, I was revisiting issues and struggles I thought I'd put behind me," she says. "For several years I had been attending every prayer workshop I could find. I had also been working at an Eastern Orthodox facility that ministered to homeless families. I was also deeply unhappy, drinking far too much and felt spiritually at home nowhere." She ended up signing up for RCIA at a parish where a friend was the director of music and liturgy, and about four months after beginning the program, she had a dream in which Mary played a memorable role. In the dream, two of her friends guided her to the parish where she was receiving her catechism. "I walked around the side of the building, which was grassy and overgrown, like an old grave-yard. As I stood by an open grave, a woman wearing a veil and long mantle appeared, hands folded in prayer as with the traditional statues of Our Lady. Slightly above her and to the side was a cloud with a hand holding a taper emerging out of it. I don't have 'big' dreams very often, but when I do I try to write them down. This was definitely one for the books."

During the ceremony of reception into the Roman Catholic church, Lucia had a moment of spiritual insight that gave her an even stronger sense of identification with Mary. "When I was anointed, God became present for me as never before—not even at Cursillo—so powerfully that for the first time I sensed dimly what it must have been like for Mary to receive the message of the angel Gabriel," she says. "In the *New American Bible* translation of the account of the anointing of the young David by the prophet Samuel, it says that from that moment 'the Spirit *rushed* upon David.' That's exactly what it felt like for me…and perhaps also for the young Mary of Nazareth?"

Reflecting on her long journey with Mary, Lucia is emphatic that Jesus' mother is not a boring Goody Two-shoes. "I don't know which is worse: the caricature of God the Father as a tyrannical old despot, or Mary as a wimpy little simpleton," she says. As proof of Mary's strong character, Lucia cites Jesus and his tenderness, patience and fierce devotion to God. Where else would those qualities come from but his own mother? "Everything I'd learned as a parent and a teacher about families and how children learn taught me that his mother was able to guide him to such a strong sense of his vocation and trust in his Father because *she demonstrated it personally*," she explains. "She taught him how to love his Father. She made it all possible, not just because she provided the human body, but because, as one of the great writers of the church expressed it, she conceived him first in her heart." As Lucia has learned, it's when we meditate on Mary's inner life that she becomes more than a plaster symbol of perfection. She becomes flesh and blood, a woman whose depth of character inspired a Savior.

* * *

Though Mary's sinlessness poses a challenge to many Catholics, another issue can be even more difficult for modern women to accept. This issue is the belief in Mary's perpetual virginity. Church tradition teaches that Mary was a virgin not only at the time of Christ's conception and birth, but that she remained chaste throughout her entire life, which means even throughout her marriage to Joseph. This teaching is reflected in much of the traditional language of the church. Every Sunday during the Nicene Creed, we affirm our belief in Jesus Christ, who was "born of the Virgin Mary"; titles such as "Blessed Virgin Mary" or "Virgin Mother" rattle instinctively off of the tongues of many Catholics. For some women, though, these titles cannot be said without feelings of discomfort, indignation or even anger. Such constant references to Mary's virginity seem to elevate that quality above all others, making it—not strength or courage or faith—her most important attribute. To many women, this feels like an admonition, as if the church is implying that the only way to be worthy is to be a virgin. Moreover, many women ask, if Mary was both a virgin *and* a mother, doesn't that make her an impossible role model? How can any other woman possibly manage to pull that off?

Caroline, a thirty-six-year-old teacher, describes her childhood image of Mary. "My impressions of Mary were that she was untouchable, superhuman, not approachable or like me at all," she recalls. As an adult, those feelings have persisted. "It seems crazy now that I don't have more of a connection to the mother of Jesus," she says. "One thing that troubles me is why the church focuses so much attention on the fact that she was a virgin. I understand trying to make the point that God the Father was the father of Jesus, but it seems to further the misconception that sex is a bad thing and that we glorify Mary in her virginity. I have a hard time with that—it takes away the very human and real aspect of Mary."

It isn't just women who struggle with Mary's perpetual virginity. Mary, a thirty-six-year-old nonprofit director, remembers being a child and asking her father if she could join in praying the rosary at her family's church. His response was, "Our family doesn't do that"—a response that only became clear to Mary later on. "In my adult years, I've learned that my father felt that the B.V.M. [Blessed Virgin Mary] gave an unhealthy perspective for women that offended him and his feminist sensibility," she says. "Yes, my dad is a feminist! Well, he probably wouldn't term it that way. But he felt the church's stance on the B.V.M. as both a virgin and a mother was an unrealistic aspiration for modern women."

Though several women had a hard time accepting Mary's virginity, others had found ways to transcend their discomfort with the "virgin label." This usually involved developing a less literal, more expansive definition of what it means to be a virgin. Beth, a forty-eight-year-old director of sales for the HBO network, offers one such perspective. "I like the idea of virginity as innocence, as openness, a womb that has not yet been filled and is open to possibility," she explains. She thinks of a virgin as "someone who has not been embittered or hurt, someone in a state of grace—which is not to say that after knowing a man one loses those things, loses grace, loses the ability to be open. I don't mean that, but [virginity] is a unique time in a woman's life." Mary's virginity also helps Beth recognize the sheer miracle of God's plan. "Imagine going from that innocence to motherhood by the Holy Spirit; it's huge," she says. "I'm still pondering it." To Beth, the very idea of virginity relates to the choices that we all face in life, choices that need to be carefully discerned in order to bring us true happiness. "Virginity is vulnerability," she says. "What you say 'yes' to can completely change your life, so you hope it'll be a good call. We all know it isn't always."

As an adult convert to Catholicism, Sarah, a musician in her early forties, has also had to wrestle with Mary's perpetual virginity. Before becoming Catholic, she felt that the emphasis on the Virgin Mary perpetuated the "Madonna/whore syndrome," sending the message that women were either "good" or they were "bad." She explains that she used to have a "stereotyped conception of Catholic men as those who would categorize women either as the girl they would want to marry—pure, submissive virgins like Mary—or the girl whom they would like to seek their pleasure with," she says. "In other words, I believed that the idolized image of the Virgin Mary served to objectify women, casting them into rigid, undeveloped, simplistic roles, the lucky ones being barefoot and pregnant in the kitchen, the unlucky ones out walking the streets."

With the passage of time, though, that belief has changed. "Life experience has filled out these perceptions for me, although I still believe that placing such emphasis on Mary's virginity fails to truly serve women," Sarah says. "More importantly, I have come to know that Mary's person encompasses infinitely more than I had originally conceived." Sarah explains that the more she has come to know Mary, the more "she has revealed herself as being powerful, strong, courageous, nurturing, loving, compassionate, peaceful and constant, to name a few. The more real she becomes the more I feel sure that she is 100 percent behind my feministic pursuits, and what's more, that she's quite confined in the role the church has designated for her."

Like Beth, Sarah has also found a more expansive way of understanding Mary's virginity: She likes to think of that virginity as "purity of heart." To her, this purity reflects Mary's infinite capacity for love. "Unconditional love is a kind of buzzword in our culture today, often used lightly," she says. "But if we truly meditate on the meaning behind those words, we find the true essence of Mary." Sarah explains that this purity of heart sets Mary apart from the rest of us, who invariably put up barriers between ourselves and others. "When you stop and think about it, is there anywhere in this world we can go to receive truly unconditional love? Mary's love is pure of heart, with no agenda, no fear, no insecurity, no jealousy, no control issues, no power-tripping—no conditions."

These insights have helped Sarah embrace Mary as a role model. Moreover, she explains that this broader definition of virginity makes Mary accessible to everyone, regardless of their sexual circumstances. "Aspiring to Mary's example of purity of heart seems a worthy goal for the celibate and non-celibate alike," she says. Seen in this light, Mary's virginity is no longer a trait that excludes. It's an invitation to all of us, a call to love as unreservedly as she does.

* * *

Not every woman who mentioned Mary's virginity saw it as a source of struggle. Sophie, a thirty-nine-year-old counselor, explains that Mary's purity is a quality she has always respected, not resented. Growing up in the Philippines, Mary was a large part of Sophie's experience of faith, and virginity was a large part of her understanding of Mary. "I thought Mary was beautiful—she looked so pure," she recalls. "Mary was to me my role model, my example." Sophie describes her childhood as being "very sheltered," and explains that she was always taught to remain chaste and save herself for marriage. She embraced the idea of sexual purity, which she explains was the norm in her culture.

When Sophie was twenty-one, she moved to the United States to attend school. The move was hard for her mother to accept. "My mom was really scared I'd lose my morals and my virginity," Sophie recalls. Even in the midst of such a secular culture, Sophie remained committed to saving herself for marriage. She began a relationship with a Protestant man who, like her, wanted to stay a virgin, and they had a chaste relationship throughout the seven years that they dated. He was accepting of Sophie's love for the Blessed Mother, even though it was foreign to his own spiritual background. "He couldn't understand my devotion to Mary, but he respected how I felt about Mary," Sophie recalls. She still has a letter that she wrote to him, in which she tried to explain the depth of her feelings for the Blessed Virgin. "It's not that I prayed to her, it's that I wanted to imitate her," Sophie says. "I felt she was perfect, beautiful."

Though Sophie and her boyfriend got engaged, she later broke off the relationship, ultimately feeing that they were not meant to be married. A month later, she moved to a large city for a new job. It was an exciting transition: She had a bigger salary and a new life. One month after her arrival, though, everything changed when she was violently raped by a stranger in the apartment where she was staying. In the space of that one event, a huge part of Sophie's self-identity was gone. "Everything—the purity, the trying to remain chaste—I'd always felt that I was doing the right thing, and in one blink of an eye, I lost it," she says. The attack was a violation not only of her identity, but also of her long-cherished hopes for the future. "I had my whole life ahead of me, and my virginity was a big part of me," she says. "I couldn't understand why it happened to me…this stranger just takes it in one instant." Following the attack, she was literally in a state of shock. Being so new to the city, she did not know where to go to report the crime. Because of her shock and horror and fear, she stayed silent. In fact, for eight years she kept quiet, telling no one what happened—not even family or friends.

The attack took a significant toll on her, both physically and emotionally. A few days after the rape, she began to feel pain, and summoned the courage to go see a doctor. She learned that she had contracted a sexually transmitted disease, a discovery that was horribly at odds with the sheltered life she'd led. "I went to the doctor, was treated, had to take an HIV test—for the first time in my life I had to learn all these things," she says. She moved out of her apartment, and later had to quit her new job because she kept crying all the time. Eventually she moved out of the city itself. Sophie also lost friendships over her experience; those who were close to her couldn't understand why she was so withdrawn.

In 2003, six years after the rape, Sophie moved back to the city where it had happened. There, she began experiencing what psychologists call "anniversary trauma." "In 2004 and 2005, I would inexplicably pass out within a month of the anniversary," she says. "In 2005, my panic attacks worsened to the point that I could barely function." This motivated her to break her long silence. She began meeting with a therapist who specialized in post-traumatic stress disorder, and started writing about the attack in a journal, "essentially reliving what happened." Both experiences were healing. Gradually, she started to share her story with loved ones, first with her mother, then with her closest friends, who were at last able to understand her behavior. "Finally, it makes sense why you were acting so crazy," one friend said.

Sophie's spirituality has also played an essential role in her healing. In November of 2005, she made a pilgrimage to Medjugorje. There, she saw a statue of Mary that moved her deeply, and affirmed the connection between the Virgin Mary and herself. "I had the feeling that though I'm not physically a virgin anymore, I'm still spiritually like her," she says. "What's more important is your heart, and I really try to strive to follow Mary in terms of humility and obedience." Sophie's lifelong love of Mary has deepened as she feels the Blessed Mother watching over her and supporting her. "Mary has been part of my healing, especially since coming back from Medjugorje. I really feel that she's protecting me, keeping me from harm," she says. On the trip, Sophie was given a special picture of Mary, which she keeps on her bedside table. "Every morning, even if I can't say anything else, I will say, 'Good morning, Blessed Mother.'" Sophie also feels supported by her own mother's devotion to Mary. Now that her mother knows about the attack, she prays specifically for her daughter's healing, a close spiritual support for which Sophie is grateful.

Though there is still a great deal of pain left from the rape, Sophie recognizes how far she has come emotionally since that day eight years ago. "To this day, I still wonder why it happened, but thank God I've been able to talk about it after eight years. It's only through the grace of God that I've been OK. I still think it's evil, but maybe there's a grace to it." Reflecting on her experience, Sophie is thankful that she did not respond to the trauma by throwing away her deeply held values and living a sexualized life. "One thing I learned is that even if it happens to you, you don't have to give up and think you've lost everything; you can still keep yourself whole," she says. She's also learned what it means to integrate life's worst experiences into one's spiritual framework: "I think faith is all about living in ambiguity and uncertainty, trusting that all will be well." It's not easy to share her story, but Sophie is aware that doing so can offer hope to other women who have suffered the same experience, showing them that healing does come in its own time. "Maybe that's the grace, to help other people," she says.

* * *

Sophie's story points to the benefit of regarding virginity in broader, more expansive terms. After all, not every woman will live a life of perpetual celibacy. Many are called to marriage, finding joy in a committed sexual relationship. Even women who do aspire to celibacy sometimes find that virginity, in its literal sense, can be taken from them by force. That's why there's a value in looking at virginity not as a physical state, but as an emotional one. If we consider the spiritual attributes that lie underneath Mary's purity, we find a host of qualities that can't be so easily violated: openness, radical trust in God, dedication to a cause the world might not understand and an essential hopefulness that remains whole, even in the face of cruelty and pain. These are qualities that all women can strive to emulate, whatever our sexual circumstances might be. When we do, it's clear that we're not so different from Mary after all. We find that every one of us can be what she was: a woman who knew herself, stood her ground and loved her God.

BRING FLOWERS OF THE FAIREST: CELEBRATING MARY

Oh Mary, we crown thee with blossoms today!
Queen of the Angels, Queen of the May!
—Traditional hymn[1]

When I entered St. Simon
Elementary School in the second grade, it felt rather like entering a new
world. There were the royal blue uniforms that all the students were
required to wear, a huge change from the lax dress code at my public elementary school. There were the nuns, with their navy habits and the sil-
ver crucifixes that swayed as they bent over our desks to offer help. There
were First Friday Masses, when the entire school gathered in the church to
pray and sing. And there was Mary.

I'd had very little contact with Mary prior to entering the school, but
it quickly became apparent that she was someone special. On that first day
in Sister Agnes's classroom, my attention was captivated by the bulletin
board on the left side of the room. It featured a drawing of a young girl
with straight dark hair, her face tilted to heaven, her expression radiant.
Sister had decorated the poster with construction-paper petals, each one
bearing a different word of a prayer I would come to know well: Hail
Mary, full of grace. Mary also stood in the corner of the classroom, a three-
dimensional statue on a small pedestal, her arms open and inviting.
Clearly, Mary was a woman worth honoring.

Later that year, I was introduced to an entirely new way to celebrate
Mary. In the spring, the student body began preparations for the annual
May procession. We spent hours practicing May songs; we brought flow-
ers from our backyards to put at the feet of the Mary statue in the church.
On the day itself, we second-graders came to school with our First

Communion clothes, worn so proudly a few weeks earlier. I remember that girls changed into our white dresses and veils in one of the second-grade classrooms, the boys having been sent to the other to put on their dress shirts and ties.

I fell in love with the May procession that year. I loved the solemnity of the long walk through the parking lot, around the church and down the center aisle toward the big statue of Mary, which was placed front and center on the altar. I adored the Mary songs we sang: "Immaculate Mary, your praises we sing," "Bring Flowers of the Fairest," and one that became a personal favorite:

> As the rain rushes down, and the earth blossoms forth,
> And the wind caresses every tree
> You can hear the turtledove singing all throughout the land
> Of the fair young Virgin Mary. [2]

Every year, I loved seeing Mary surrounded by the flowers we'd brought, the mismatched floral offerings that somehow looked beautiful together. It was always a thrill to see Mary crowned with the wreath that had been carried down the aisle by a lucky little girl. Though I couldn't have articulated it at the time, there was an innocence, a fundamental hopefulness to the procession that always made me happy. For a few hours, we were putting aside our books and spelling lists and math tests and focusing on the celebration of beauty. We were honoring the woman on the altar, a woman whose outer loveliness was but a hint of what was inside.

* * *

Over the past few years, I've reflected often on the importance of celebrations, both religious and secular. I've come to the conclusion that celebrations are an essential part of a happy life. Whether they are birthdays, graduation parties, wedding or baby showers, celebrations help us refocus our attention on what really matters. Though these events often center on a specific achievement—finishing college, say, or an impending birth— they are primarily a celebration of a person. When friends gather for a birthday party, it's not so much about marking the passage of another year as it is about honoring the friend in question. It's about showing this person that we love him or her enough to respond to an invitation, to buy a card or a gift, to get dressed up, to get into the car. "We value your presence in our lives," these celebrations say. "We'd rather be here with you than anywhere else."

Looking back, I can see that those childhood May processions helped me understand the value of spending time with Mary. The hours of practicing, the flowers brought from home, the little loving touches—they all spoke to the high esteem and affection that the sisters and teachers felt for Mary. Their enthusiasm was contagious. Every year, from second grade to eighth, I adored being part of the beautiful celebration.

My fondness for May processions is hardly unique. Many women shared similar stories, speaking of childhood Marian celebrations with affection and warmth. Like me, Jean, a sixty-seven-year-old retired junior high school teacher, has the sisters to thank for her exposure to Mary. "My childhood impressions of her were formed in elementary school by the Sisters of Charity and have remained with me all these years," she says. Jean recalls the excitement she used to feel during the annual classroom celebrations of Mary. "My memories go back to my desire to make a rose crown for Mary during the month of May. We would crown her each day in class and sing a hymn to her name. There was a white rosebush on my porch at home and I couldn't wait for the roses to blossom so that I could be the one bringing in the crown."

Andrea, a thirty-five-year-old eating disorder activist, remembers the impressions of Mary that were formed during her first grade year. "There was a beautiful statue of her in the church that stood in its very own special place, where people would place candles at her feet. I remember she was so beautiful that it made you feel all warm inside and the light that rose up from the candles made her face glow so radiantly, you just knew there was something more to her. She was peaceful." Andrea's sense that Mary was special was affirmed by the school's annual May crownings. It was a day that Andrea always anticipated with great excitement. "A few special little girls wore these lovely light blue dresses, while one eighth-grader was chosen to crown Mary with a wreath of flowers as we sang a hymn of praise to honor her. Pastel-colored ribbons flowed from the crown as it lay on a special pillow that the young girl carried up the long church aisle. I dreamt of one day being that eighth-grader."

May processions are not the only way to honor Mary. Dolores, who has a long-standing devotion to Mary, describes the many rituals that have made Jesus' mother such an important part of her life. The seventy-year-old retired nurse and teacher has fond memories of Mary celebrations at her childhood parish. "I recall being part of the annual May crowning celebrations where the church was packed with Mary's devotees as well as my being included in the living rosaries held on the church grounds," she says. "Novenas to Our Blessed Mother and the Litany of the Blessed Virgin Mary were regular prayer events that were said not only during the month of May and October but throughout the year." High school also provided Dolores with ample opportunities to honor Mary. "Annual retreats held during the school year often centered around Mary, and the annual crowning of the Queen of May brought a court of gowned classmates to Mary's shrine—an honor to be selected a member of the court." As a teenager, Dolores also became a member of the Children of Mary, a worldwide organization devoted to Jesus' mother. She joined others in celebrating the Blessed Mother at the Third Marian Regional Congress in Utica, New York, in 1951, where she was "fully engaged as one of Mary's clients."

With these early experiences of Mary, it's not surprising that Dolores has been close to the Blessed Mother throughout her adult life. After graduating from high school, Dolores entered a Catholic nursing school. "I have always felt that my nursing training was enhanced because of Mary's intercession and that my years of nursing experience were guided by her," she says. It isn't just Dolores's professional life that has been touched by Mary's care. "My now twenty-seven-year-old son was conceived during my forty-second year, and Mary was surely with me during those nine months of waiting," she says. "I thank her for an uncomplicated pregnancy and delivery, and for our beautiful child."

Though Dolores has participated in numerous public celebrations of Mary, she honors her in quiet, personal ways, too. "I have several favorite Mary commemoratives which I display with pride—a Hummel statue of Mary and Child, given to each nursing graduate from the nuns of my nursing school; a statue of the Pietà, recalling for me Mary's profound grief at her Son's death, and a tall satin-white statue of Mary made during my 'ceramic' days." These statues are tangible illustrations of the love and respect that Dolores feels for Mary. "I call upon Our Blessed Mother in good times and in bad, and although I have not had any Mary sightings or revelations or anything out of the ordinary, she is with me each and every day," she says.

Like Dolores, Mary, a sixty-two-year-old retired teacher, cherishes her close relationship with the Blessed Mother. "I am the Blessed Virgin Mary's biggest fan," she says. "I cannot imagine my life without having the ability to call upon her twenty times daily." It's a relationship that Mary learned from her own mother. "My mother also loved Mary. When things were difficult, she'd say, 'I just can't take care of this now. I put it in the hands of the Blessed Mother.' " More than an intercessor, the Blessed Mother is also Mary's personal guide on how to live. "She has always been my model—how to treat others as a friend, as a teacher, as a mother."

Mary's lifelong love of the mother of Jesus infuses the springtime with joy and meaning. "I've always loved the month of May because of Mary," she explains. Over the years, Mary has created a lovely tradition of her own: the celebration of the Blessed Mother inside her home. "Each year to date I've had Mary-lovers like myself come over and we've sung the old May songs: 'Tis the Month of our Mother,' 'On this Day, O Beautiful Mother,' 'Bring Flowers of the Fairest.' " One of Mary's friends has helped facilitate the celebration by compiling a booklet of all the classic May songs.

Just as her own mother modeled the importance of having such a powerful intercessor, Mary has done what she can to make the Blessed Mother a household name within her own family. "I cannot imagine my life without the comfort and solace of Mary. I am so grateful that I have this relationship," she explains. "Because I feel so strongly about this, I worked really hard to instill it in our children. I think most of them [have it]." As Mary's experiences show, a love for the Blessed Mother doesn't have to begin in a parish or a school. It can blossom right at home, fed by prayer and nurtured by song.

* * *

Though American celebrations of Mary tend to take place within a home, school or church, other countries honor Mary on a much larger scale. In some cultures, the celebration of the Blessed Mother even becomes the focal point of the entire community, stopping traffic and drawing sizable crowds. Maria, a thirty-four-year-old who works for a non-profit organization, describes the famous Holy Week processions in her native Guatemala. Unlike the May processions, which honor beauty and new life, these Holy Week processions highlight another aspect of Mary's story—her sorrow.

In the processions, large wooden stands bearing statues of Mary and Jesus are carried slowly through the streets. "It's very solemn," Maria explains. "There's always a big band accompanying the procession—first goes Jesus, then Mary." Traditionally, men carry the image of Christ and women shoulder the armoire holding Mary. There is incense, and carpets of flowers and fruit are laid out in the streets, which are closed to cars. The processions can be up to twelve hours long, often continuing throughout the night.

In 2002, Maria participated in the processions for the first time, one of anywhere from twenty-five to fifty women who support the sorrowful Mary in her long walk through the streets. It's not easy; the women are dressed in their best clothes, often wearing high heels, which make it challenging to carry the image of Mary through the cobblestone streets.

The armoire itself is "heavy, heavy, heavy," she says. "At times, you're crying, 'Relieve me,' but we do this for the devotion of Mary." Maria discovered, though, that there's an emotion that helps transcend the pain. "I remember my sister and I just tearing up and feeling this overwhelming sense of joy and happiness and peace, just being touched by the whole experience."

Since that first year, Maria has made a point of returning to Guatemala each year to participate in the processions. It's a trip that flows out of her love for the Blessed Mother, who has always been a close maternal figure in her life. "Mary is like the ultimate mother. I've always been in love with her, very close to her apparitions and messages." Maria explains that she's always been surrounded by women who love Mary, including her mother and grandmother. In fact, the women in Maria's family have given her a particular context for understanding Mary. "Latin women tend to be the focus, the strength of a family—Mary was that as well," she says. While fathers are the ones who give directions, "mothers tend to be the ones who console, who embrace." The maternal comfort that Mary gives is an essential part of Maria's faith life. "If anybody ever tried to convert me to another religion, I couldn't do it because of my love of Mary," she says. "How could you give her up? I could never give her up." Though she sometimes feels guilty about not praying more to Jesus, she knows that God approves of her affection for the Blessed Mother. "God gave her to us—he instructed that this woman would be important to us. We didn't make it up," she says. "Jesus listens to her. She's a true intercessor for us. She's our Mama."

* * *

As I know from my St. Simon days, there's a power in being exposed to Marian celebrations at a young age. Those early memories of the flower-filled church and the Mary songs have stayed fresh in my mind throughout the years. Even in college and my early twenties, when I felt the most distant from Mary, I still thought of the May processions with a warmth that little else in my Catholic past could generate. Something in these rituals, it seems, can captivate the childhood imagination like little else.

That's why it was fascinating for me to hear the perspective of Linda, my mother, a sixty-two-year-old convert to Catholicism. Unlike me, her first significant exposure to Mary did not come until she was an adult. Prior to writing this book, I'd never had any particular reason to ask her about Mary, so I was curious to find out what role the Blessed Mother played in her life. On a road trip to visit my sister, I peppered her with questions, and learned some surprising things about my mother's journey with Mary.

As a child, my mother grew up in Unity Church, a Protestant denomination. "Mary was not a part of Unity Church," my mother explains. "She was only there as the mother of Jesus, but it ended there." Other than the statue in the family Christmas crèche, my mom remembers almost no childhood exposure to Mary. "If anything, I had more negative vibes from some of my anti-Catholic relatives," she remembers. Her grandmother, a staunch Scottish Presbyterian, had many "very dated Catholic notions." She was so upset by the election of John F. Kennedy as president that she even refused to watch Jacqueline Kennedy's much-anticipated television tour of the White House. When my mother got engaged to my father, a Catholic, it was, she recalls, "quite something." When her grandmother actually met my father, though, her views began to relax. "I could see her gradually start to thaw," says my mother. She later wrote my mother a letter in which she praised my father as "a nice young man."

Even so, the introduction to my father's faith was an adjustment. One of the first differences my mother noticed was the decor of my dad's church. "Unity Church has such an absence of icons and statues," my mother explains. "There weren't even any crosses in the churches, only flowers and podiums." The first time my mother attended Mass with my father, she recalls being shocked by the statues of Mary and the saints, which to her seemed "superstitious." "It felt very foreign to me at first. I thought, 'Are these people worshipping these statues?'"

It was a conversation with my paternal grandmother, my Grandma Kubitz, that helped my mother see Mary in a more personal light. My grandmother had always had a strong affection for Mary, one that dated from her childhood in a convent school outside of Chicago. When she married my grandfather, she made the Blessed Mother a part of the ceremony by lighting a candle at the Mary statue and saying a prayer. She always felt that Mary had given their marriage a special blessing. A few years after my parents were married, Grandma shared this cherished memory with my mother. "My reaction was, 'Oh, that was really wonderful,' though I had no connection to Mary myself," my mom recalls. "I thought it was a nice feminine touch to add to the wedding. I was kind of envious in a way," she adds. "It made me feel that I wish I'd had something that gave me such a blessing."

Several years later, when my sister and I entered St. Simon's, my mother attended the school's May procession. Like me, she was struck by the loveliness of the event. "I thought that was one of the most beautiful celebrations." She was taken with the solemn way in which the students processed into the church, with the flowers, with the crowds of parents and grandparents and younger siblings who came to watch the celebration and to honor Mary.

As our family became more involved in the school and the parish, my mother felt a growing pull to become a Catholic. In 1983, she entered RCIA and was received into the church the following spring. One year later, she began teaching at St. Simon's and she remained on staff until her recent retirement. As a teacher, she came to love the school's annual May traditions. "As soon as May begins, every classroom has a bulletin board dedicated to Mary. There are beautiful bulletin boards in the hall, fresh flowers by the Mary statue. It seems comforting to see all those Mary touches. I feel peaceful when I look at them, when I look at a nice tribute to Mary." She's as captivated by the May procession now as she was the first time she witnessed it years ago. She speaks fondly of the moment when the eighth grade forms an honor guard down the middle of the church and a trio of second graders walks the floral crown to the statue on the altar. "When I see Mary with the wreath on her head and hear the singing, I always get a lump in my throat and tears in my eyes," she says. "It's a beautiful moment." As a teacher, she has had an insider's perspective on the way the event comes together, and has always been moved by the message behind all the careful preparations. "I like the fact that the children are told that this is our gift to Mary, that our behavior, our reverence, is a gift to Mary," she says. "I think that's what I like—a sense of giving your complete best to Mary." She's also pleased that people who happen to be driving by the church can see the students, clean and spruced up, processing and singing. "It sends nice memories to people who are Catholic, and people who aren't Catholic can't help but be struck by the solemnity of it all."

Though my mother says she doesn't pray through Mary, she understands the appeal of doing so. "It gives people a lot of comfort. It puts the feminine into the prayers." Her primary image of Mary is of a woman being celebrated, honored, surrounded by flowers and beauty. It's an image that, in its own way, helps bring her closer to God himself. "The Mary/flower connection is important to me," she says. "The beauty of Mary and the beauty of the flowers point to the beautiful creation of God." And though she once associated Mary statues with superstition, those days have passed. Thanks to the loving tributes of a school community, images of the Blessed Mother now evoke a deeper, more positive feeling. "Mary represents so much peace," she says simply. "When I look at her, I feel peaceful."

* * *

My mother and I are fortunate to have had these experiences. Though May processions were commonplace fifty years ago, the tradition has fallen off over the past several decades. As a result, many Catholics of my generation have never had the opportunity to participate in these rituals. It's a shame, for I know from personal experience that celebrations like these can be the first step of a journey into knowing and loving Mary.

When we see a woman being crowned with flowers, honored in a shrine in a neighbor's home, or carried through the streets by dedicated crowds, we can't help but wonder what it is about her that inspires such devotion. And while it's true that usually we celebrate the people we love, the witness of many women indicates that sometimes, the reverse is just as true. Sometimes, we come to love the people we celebrate.

But Mary treasured all these words, and pondered them in her heart.
(Luke 2:19)

"A few months ago, I was waiting for a program to begin at my parish, Most Holy Redeemer in San Francisco," says Edna, a thirty-three-year-old retail operations associate. "I saw a young man wearing a raglan shirt, white background and black three-quarter-length sleeves. The shirt had a silk-screened image of the Virgin Mary and her loving smile and demure pose. Underneath the image, there were the words, 'Mary Is My Homegirl.'"

The shirt made Edna smile. Having grown up west of Los Angeles, in a city with a large Latino population, she was well acquainted with the term. "In the Mexican-American street culture, a homegirl, or its male counterpart, homeboy, was a term reserved for your closest friends. A homegirl was someone who was there for you as a friend, an advocate, a parental figure, someone who spoke on your behalf, someone you respect," she explains. "She will take you and love you despite your faults and failings. She might be irritated by them but a true homegirl would be the one to bring out the best of you and love you for who you are. She is respected by your friends, your neighbors, your enemies, your family. She has utter and complete faith in you and love for you." As far as Edna was concerned, the term was perfectly fitting. "The description of a homegirl sounds familiar. She sounds like someone we know. Doesn't she sound like, well, the Blessed Mother?"

One woman's Holy Virgin is another woman's homegirl. In writing this book, I've been blessed to see, firsthand, how wonderfully universal Mary is. There's no one single image of Mary that speaks to women today, and in this lies her power. She's the woman with a thousand faces and a thousand titles, transcending the boundaries of culture and age. She also walks with us on our individual journeys, engaging with us in any number of different ways as our life circumstances shift and change. If I've learned anything from the stories in this book, I've learned that you never can know exactly when or how Mary will come to meet you. You never can predict when or how she'll show up, smiling with gentle recognition, taking up residence in your heart.

As I wrote the last few chapters of this book, a blessed event occurred in my own life. I gave birth to a son, Matthew, the answer to so many prayers. With his arrival, everything in my life is different. There are the expected changes, of course—the sleepless nights, the adorable baby smiles, the fact that going down the street now requires about as much gear as going on safari. But there are other, more subtle changes too, changes that have come at me from the inside out.

For one thing, I've learned something that I only dimly knew before: Moms possess amazing depths of knowledge about their children. At this moment, I know my little boy better than he knows himself. When he's older, he won't know anything about this time in his life. He won't remember how he stared at his arm continuously one day, discovering it for the first time, a look of total absorption on his face. He won't know how he used to laugh and kick to the silly unrhymed songs I composed while changing his diapers. He won't remember that magic bath day, when he no longer screamed but instead sat quietly, looking slightly perplexed but calm, deciding that warm water is a good thing after all. He won't know these, or a thousand other little things about his early life.

But I will. And if he ever wants to know what he was like as a child, so fresh from God, he'll ask me, and I'll be able to tell him. I'm so blessed to have this beautiful knowledge, the knowledge that I treasure in my heart.

So it is with Mary and Jesus. No wonder we honor her, this privileged woman. She knew our Savior before he knew himself.

And as I hold my little son and pray for his health and safety and happiness, I sometimes think: This is how Mary held Jesus, how she looked at him, and what she hoped for him. Yes, I've been on quite a journey with Mary. She's been so many things to me: the beautiful woman crowned with flowers, the supportive cousin, the fellow mourner, the faithful intercessor. I know that my sense of her will continue to shift and change over time, because that's how she works. But at this moment in my life, this sleep-deprived moment of exhilarating new mommyhood, she's something very special. She's the young mother with a tiny baby on her lap, memorizing the way his chest rises with each breath, her heart so full of emotion it seems it will break. And in this quiet, ordinary moment, she's doing something extraordinary: She's showing Love himself what it means to be loved. "All generations shall call me blessed," she said.

Yes, indeed.

Visitation: The Journey Into Community

1. John J. Kilgallen, S.J., *A New Testament Guide to the Holy Land* (Chicago: Loyola, 1998), pp. 102–107.

Nativity: Having a Mother, Being a Mother

1. "Hosea," music and lyrics by Gregory Norbert, O.S.B., © 1972, The Benedictine Foundation of the State of Vermont, Inc.

Our Heavenly Intercessor: Praying With Mary

1. From "Behold Your Mother: Woman of Faith, A Pastoral Letter Issued by the National Conference of Catholic Bishops," November 21, 1973, in *Mary in the Church: A Selection of Teaching Documents* (Washington, D.C.: United States Conference of Catholic Bishops, 2003), p. 29.

2. From "*Rosarium Virginis Mariae:* On the Most Holy Rosary, An Apostolic Letter of His Holiness John Paul II," October 16, 2002, in *Mary in the Church: A Selection of Teaching Documents,* p. 151.

Mary of the Apparitions: A Mother Who Reaches Out

1. Quote from the *Nican Mopohua*, translated from Spanish by Virgil Elizondo, in his book *Guadalupe: Mother of the New Creation* (Maryknoll, N.Y.: Orbis, 1997), p. 8.

Immaculate Mary: Perfection and Virginity

1. "Hail Mary, Gentle Woman," text and music by Carey Landry, © 1975, 1978, Carey Landry.

Bring Flowers of the Fairest: Celebrating Mary

1. "Bring Flowers of the Rarest," traditional hymn.
2. "Magnificat," text and music by Robert Blue, © 1968, F.E.L. Publications, Ltd.

| BIBLIOGRAPHY |

Chiffolo, Anthony F. *100 Names of Mary*. Cincinnati: St. Anthony Messenger Press, 2002.

Elizondo, Virgil. *Guadalupe: Mother of the New Creation*. Maryknoll, N.Y.: Orbis, 1997.

Kilgallen, John J., S.J., *A New Testament Guide to the Holy Land*. Chicago: Loyola, 1998.

United States Conference of Catholic Bishops. *Mary in the Church: A Selection of Teaching Documents*. Washington, D.C.: United States Conference of Catholic Bishops, 2003.